WARBIRDTECH SERIES

VOLUME 15

NORTHROP
P-61 BLACK WIDOW

BY WARREN E. THOMPSON

specialtypress

PUBLISHERS AND WHOLESALERS

Published by
Specialty Press Publishers and Wholesalers
11481 Kost Dam Road
North Branch, MN 55056
United States of America
(612) 583-3239

Distributed in the UK and Europe by
Airlife Publishing Ltd.
101 Longden Road
Shrewsbury
SY3 9EB
England

ISBN 0-933424-80-9

Designed by Greg Compton

Printed in the United States of America

TABLE OF CONTENTS

THE NORTHROP P-61 BLACK WIDOW

FOREWORD **4**
BY JOHN W. MYERS, TEST PILOT FOR NORTHROP ON THE P-61

PREFACE **5**
IN 1941, THE NEED FOR A NIGHT FIGHTER WAS CRITICAL

CHAPTER 1: CREATING THE BLACK WIDOW **6**
NORTHROP'S ENGINEERS FILL THE GAP IN SHORT ORDER

CHAPTER 2: OPERATIONAL TEST & EVALUATION **14**
ARMY AIR CORPS TEST PILOTS IRON OUT THE WRINKLES

CHAPTER 3: ANATOMY OF THE P-61 . . . . **20**
RIVETS, WIRING AND SPARS COME TOGETHER TO FORM THE BLACK WIDOW

CHAPTER 4: FLYING THE P-61 . . . . **42**
HIGHLY SKILLED CREW MAKE THE WIDOW STING

CHAPTER 5: ARMAMENT AND RADAR **60**
THE P-61'S NIGHT VISION AND FIREPOWER HAD NO EQUAL

SPECIAL FULL COLOR SECTION: FRAMED IN FULL COLOR **65**
THE NOCTURNAL HUNTER IS CAPTURED WITH KODACHROME

CHAPTER 6: NORTHROPS HOT RODS **78**
THE P-61C, D AND E: A BETTER MOUSETRAP IS DEVELOPED, BUT THE WAR ENDS

CHAPTER 7: THE FINAL CHAPTER **88**
THE JET AGE CUTS THE WIDOW'S CAREER SHORT

APPENDIX **99**
NORTHROP P-61 PRODUCTION STATISTICS

SIGNIFICANT DATES **100**
KEY DATES IN THE HISTORY OF THE P-61 BLACK WIDOW

WARBIRDTECH
S E R I E S

FOREWORD

BY JOHN W. MYERS, TEST PILOT FOR NORTHROP ON THE P-61

While serving as a Lockheed Company production test pilot, I had a field day flying Lockheed 10s, 12s, Lodestars, Venturas and the "Yippee" (the YP-38 accelerated service test) airplanes. I must confess, though, that my only major contribution to any of these programs was that I introduced Tony LeVier to the P-38.

In 1941, I received an invitation from Mr. Jack Northrop, who had left Douglas to form his own company, to call upon him. He offered me the job of chief test pilot with the new Northrop Company, and I was still retained by Lockheed to test some of their aircraft. Talk about a kid in a candy store!

Vance Breese, who was at that time the country's best-known test pilot, had made the first and only flight on the XP-61 and had recommended me for follow up tests. My check out in the XP-61 was only a few minutes in the cockpit.

Test pilot John W. Myers walks away from one of the advanced P-61C models after a test flight. Myers was involved in all of the testing of the Northrop night fighters from the early tests until the war ended. (John Myers)

My first flight pointed out one immediate concern: unstable pitch. The airplane had been designed to have full-span double-slotted flaps, with spoilers for lateral control (low landing speed being much desired for a night fighter). In wind tunnel tests, the negative pitching movement created by these enormous flaps, dictated that massive down loads would be required on the tail, so the hinge line of the elevator had to be located several inches above the horizontal tail. In the wind tunnel, though, there were lateral control problems, so the flight test airplane originally had no flaps and had conventional ailerons, but it did have that very high elevator hinge line. And, boy, was it unstable to pitch.

After my second flight, I asked the engineering department to move the pitch trim wheel so that it was next to the throttles, giving me a better chance to keep forces down to a level I could control. It sure made me wish that I had four hands.

At this time, there was no better engine than the Pratt & Whitney and the Black Widow received one: an 18 cylinder P&W R2800 with 2,800 cubic inches and 2,400 horsepower. The engines on the Black Widow were the first to have a two-speed, two-stage, gear-driven supercharger. I came back to base numerous times with one engine in pieces because a master rod would fail and take all the articulating rods with it. With that airplane, such an event was a "ho hum." It turned out that the master piston pin was starving for oil.

Once the tests were over, I was sent out to the forward bases during the war to teach the young pilots how to get the most out of the P-61. Naturally, they thought there was no way a 35,000 pound fighter could be maneuverable and were greatly concerned about loss of control in the event of an engine failure. I had practiced a "show off" flight that took about three minutes. I did a very short take-off roll, back across the deck at red-line (420 MPH), loop down to deck again and Immelmann. Coming out of the Immelmann, I feather one engine on the way down to the deck, then did two slow rolls off the deck into the dead engine, approach and land short.

My own objective during testing was to make this lethal weapon (four 20MM cannon and four .50-caliber machine guns), the easiest to fly, most forgiving airplane in history, so that those kids who were going to fly it on a black night would have every comfort and every aid we could give them. And we did. I honestly believe that we made it the safest, most forgiving fighter of its size ever built!

JOHN W. MYERS
May 15, 1997

PREFACE

In 1941, the need for a night fighter was critical.

The purpose of this book is to take a look at the Northrop P-61 Black Widow from a slightly different angle. This aircraft was a complex, state-of-the-art fighter that had an extremely short life span of only five years from conception to mothballs. Its specialty was hunting at night and its success in this area had a profound effect on enemy activities after dark.

During its brief history, the Black Widow and its aircrews wrote the manual on "Night Fighter/All-Weather Tactics." The basics of this doctrine would be valid well into the years when jets dominated the all-weather business.

The P-61 made such a significant impact in a short period of time for a combination of reasons, in particular, the highly skilled pilot/radar observer team and the immense firepower that this fighter brought into the arena. The Black Widow had four .50-caliber machine guns mounted on the top of the crew nacelle and four fixed 20MM cannon in its belly. These straight-forward firing guns were capable of spewing out more destruction than any American fighter built during the war rivaling the P-47 that with its eight .50-calibers was one of the most lethal fighters to emerge from World War II.

After the cloak of secrecy was removed and the public became aware of the Black Widow's presence, the news media described it as looking like an overgrown P-38. Once more details were released and some of its statistics published, though, it was obvious that Northrop had built the largest fighter to come out of World War II and perhaps the most deadly.

In the spring of 1941, the United States was observing the war in Europe—from a distance. The Germans were proving to be unbeatable and their development of night flying tactics was taking a heavy toll on England, 24 hours a day. In turn, the British were forced to develop a very effective night fighter program. Unknown to the United States, the British were gaining knowledge, which would soon be passed on to the Army Air Corps.

The United States realized the need for a pure-bred night fighter in early 1940. Northrop had begun designing the P-61 in November 1940, and the contract for two experimental models was signed in January 1941. The first XP-61 was test flown on May 26, 1942, but deliveries to the AAC did not commence until July 1943.

Naturally, there were problems, but that is the way it was (and still is) with sophisticated new aircraft, especially those with advanced equipment and the P-61 had more state-of-the- art features than any fighter to emerge during the war years. As the pages in this book will show, the Black Widow was an engineering marvel, slightly ahead of its time. One Northrop official stated, "The P-61 has all of the refinements necessary to be the best night fighter in the business." If you had to accurately describe this aircraft in one sentence, it would read: The Northrop P-61 Black Widow is a very unconventional design and has enormous horsepower complemented by unbelievable firepower.

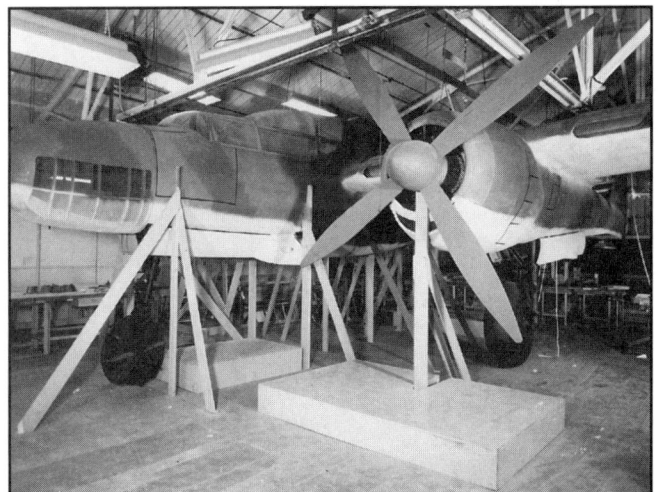

It is hard to believe that this mock-up of the P-61 was built nine months before the Japanese attack on Pearl Harbor. The Northrop engineers put this together to make sure the configuration was what the military wanted. The only major change was moving the 20MM cannon from the wing area to the bottom of the crew nacelle. (Gerald Balzer)

CREATING THE BLACK WIDOW

The raging war over the skies of England in 1940 made the front pages of most every newspaper in the world. What didn't get much attention was the fact that the Germans had made impressive improvements in their ability to fly at night, which were being painfully manifested over London.

The U.S. Army Air Corps had noted this efficiency, and Jack Northrop was contacted early on to design and build a night fighter that would be an effective defensive deterrent against this type of warfare. Based on British input and suggestions of Army Air Corps personnel who had witnessed the Battle of Britain, the image of the American night

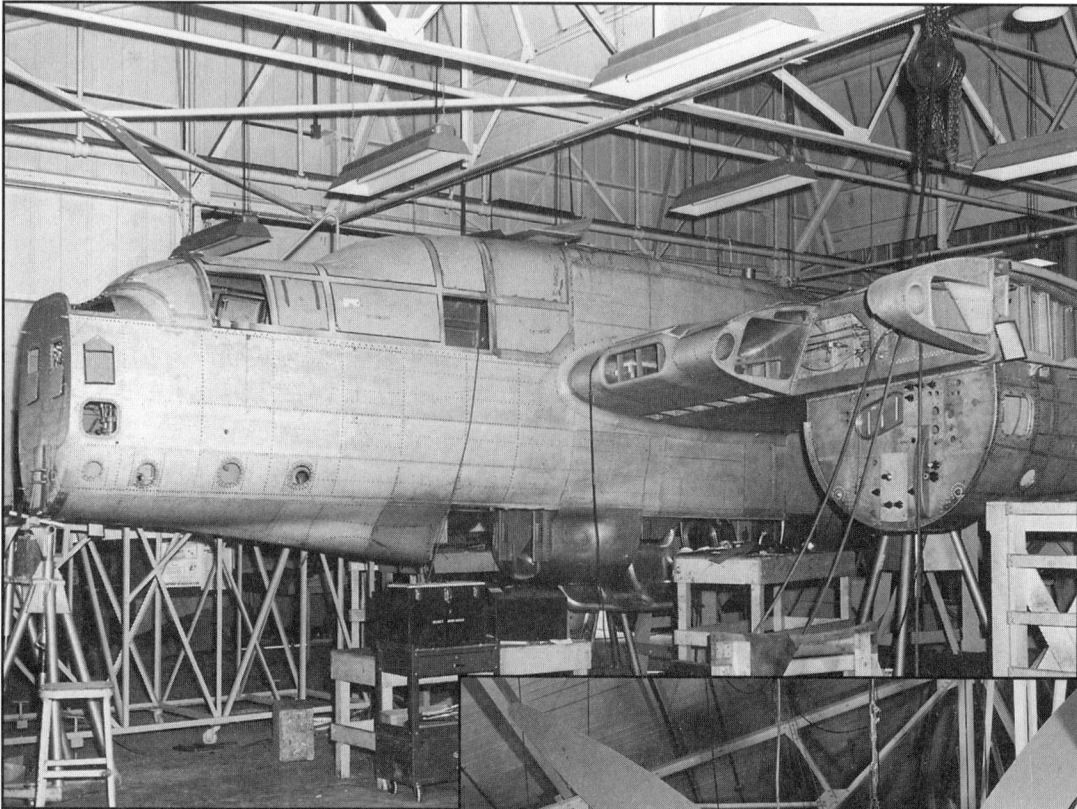

(Above) The second of two XP-61s is assembled at the Northrop plant. The engine nacelles were being attached to the crew nacelle. This XP was AF Serial # 41-19510. (Roy Wolford)

In 1941, 26 experts from the Army, Navy and Royal Air Force flew out to the Northrop plant in California to inspect the completed mock-up. It passed muster and the detail planners began the tedious work of preparing to build the two XP-61 models. This view is from the front of the left engine nacelle. (Gerald Balzer)

WARBIRD**TECH** SERIES

fighter shaped up. Among the more dominant features that the airframe was required to have were lethal armament, extensive loiter time, state-of-the-art radar. It not only must have an effective defensive capability, but be able to go on the offensive as well. It had to have speed, yet be able to slow down to a crawl. The take-off roll must be short, allowing it to operate off the crude, short airstrips found in forward areas. With the proper flaps, it should be able to land at very slow speeds, allowing it to recover on those short strips.

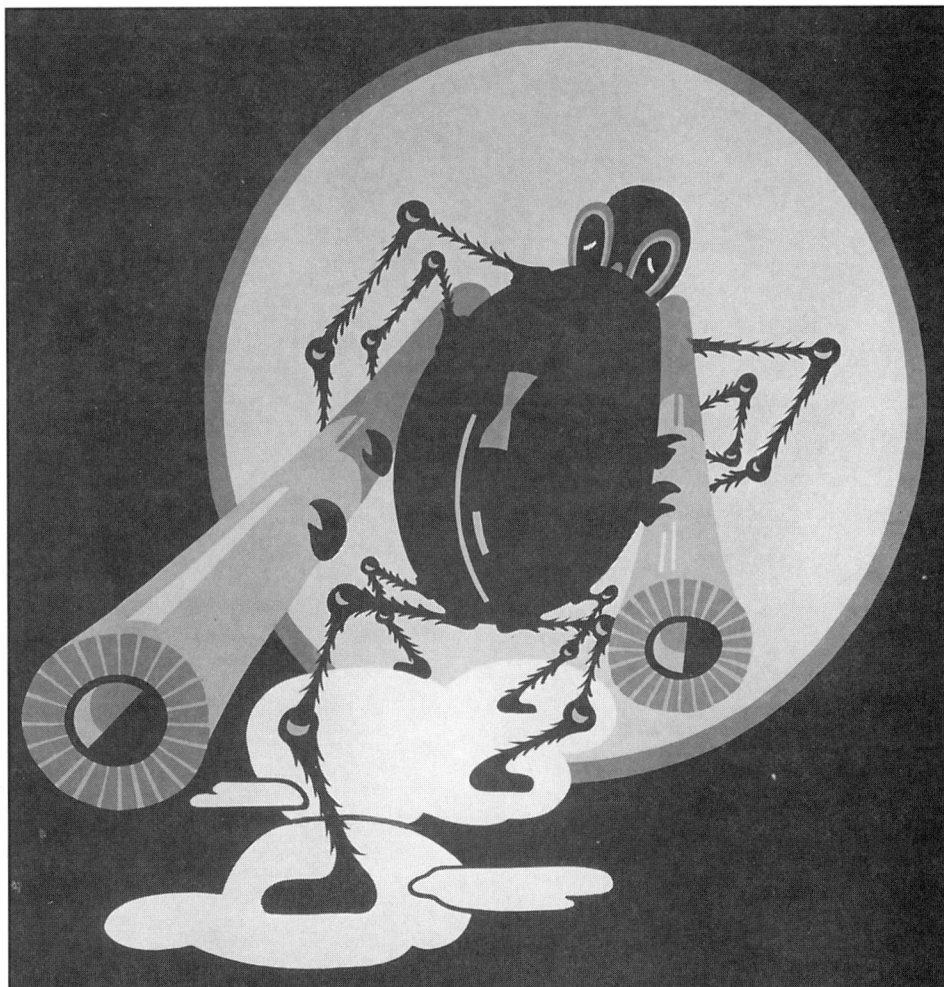

Perhaps, the most important ideas for the new aircraft were based on its operational capability from forward landing fields, which provided a new dimension in protecting the front line troops and supplies at night. If the new design could move as the front lines moved, then the risks of enemy aircraft attacking friendly troops

Aircraft #703 was built as a static test bed for the upcoming production of 13 YP-61's. This picture shows work being done on the cannon fairings and access panels to the ventral area of the crew nacelle. (Northrop)

5225-013 NORTHROP
STATIC SHIP #703. CANNON FAIRING INSTALL XP61

The first XP-61 to roll out of the factory gets a final check before undergoing flight testing. The first flight of an XP-61 was in May 1942. One of most noticeable changes that would take place between this model and the production A models was the shape of the canopy. Also note the early AAF insignia on the engine nacelle. (Gerald Balzer/Northrop)

Lieutenant Colonel Marshall Roth, Wright Army Air Field's project officer, sits in the front seat of an XP-61. Behind him is Northrop test pilot John W. Myers. It was Myers who familiarized most of the high-ranking AAC officers with the P-61. (Gerald Balzer)

and supply lines at night diminished significantly. The closer to the front lines the new night fighter could operate, the more loiter time it had over friendly forces.

Acceptance by both the Army and Navy was a tedious ordeal that was required of every proposed aircraft design. However, after numerous meetings and many months of planning, the P-61's creation was close at hand. The situation in England continued to deteriorate and the urgent need to design and produce the night fighter escalated.

Both XP-61 models (#41-19509 and #41-19510) and a static test model (#703) are shown during the building process at the Northrop plant. The first flight of the XP-61 would take place shortly after the roll-out May 1942. (Roy Wolford)

WARBIRD**TECH**
S E R I E S

A scale drawing of the first production XP-61(#41-19509) shows the exact proportion of the average size pilot with the Black Widow. This illustrates just how large the airframe was and how the P-61 earned the distinction of the being the largest fighter produced in the United States during the war. (Gerald Balzer/Northrop)

A good three-quarter rear view of the first finished XP-61 after it had rolled out of the plant. Both of the XPs were equipped with the top .50-caliber turret. Based on how well the XP looked on paper, the Army Air Corps officials went ahead and ordered the 13 YP-61s that were produced. This was not standard procedure, but the night fighter was desperately needed. (Roy Wolford)

The conferences and meetings that concerned Northrop's development of the required night fighter did not begin until November 1940. On January 30, 1941, Northrop and the Army Air Corps signed a formal contract totalling $1,367,000 that included two experimental aircraft (XP-61s) and two wind tunnel models. Northrop's engineers built a full-scale wooden mock-up of the XP-61. When this was completed, 26 experts from the Army, Navy and Royal Air Force flew out to look over the model. They were so favorably impressed with what the XP-61 looked like, on paper, that Northrop received the green light to proceed with the production of 13 YP-61s.

So, on March 10, just 38 days after the initial contract for the YP-61 was signed, another contract was approved by the under secretary of war for five and one-half million dollars. This ensured the production of 13 YP-61s, and the groundwork was laid for the production of the airframes that would become the famous P-61 Black Widows.

Early in the design of the night fighter, two options were considered, one with twin booms and one with a single tail. Obviously, the one with the twin engine nacelles won out. The final okay also included two 2,000-horsepower radial air-cooled engines.

This photograph was taken on February 12, 1942, at the Northrop plant. Nine weeks after the United States entered the war, the first XP-61 was taking shape. The crew nacelle in the background is probably the second prototype XP. (Gerald Balzer/Northrop)

This scene is well into the mass production period of the P-61. These are B models which differ from the A models in that the length of the nose cone was extended to house the new, upgraded radar unit and they were fitted with built-in night binoculars for the pilot.
(Roy Wolford)

The rapid series of events that followed the late 1940 conferences were, by no means the accepted procedure on new aircraft designs and production. The urgency of the concept and the excellent job that had been done by the Northrop people led to the unusual series of contracts being signed in a short period of time, culminating with one for several hundred Black Widows, which was signed on February 28, 1942. Most of this took place

before the United States had entered the war.

The P-61 design, with the exception of full-span flaps, spoiler-type ailerons and booster-type elevator

In this scene toward the final stages of the production line, there are almost enough P-61Bs in this picture to outfit an entire night fighter squadron. The engines have been installed, and on the left are the props and spinners that will be the next item to be married up with airframe. The P-61B-15 models started receiving the top turrets again.
(Roy Wolford)

Three models of the P-61 were built for extensive testing in wind tunnels. Their sizes varied from a 1/8 to a 1/20 to a 1/30 scale. The 1/8 was tested in the wind tunnel facility at the California Institute of Technology. (Gerald Balzer)

The second production XP-61 runs up its engines for the studio cameras at Culver City, California. It was a key figure in a training film produced by the First Motion Picture Unit for the U.S. Signal Corps. With no markings and the all-black paint scheme, it was an ominous looking aircraft. (USAF)

A one-quarter left rear angle of the Static XP-61 model that was built (ship # 703). (Gerald Balzer)

tabs, had a conventional design. The exceptional flaps gave the heavy fighter an official landing speed of about 80 MPH (published). Actually, many pilots stated they had landed it on short strips in the forward areas, at speeds of 70 MPH and under.

In an initial evaluation report, one of the items listed that needed improvement was to find a better flame damper for the exhausts. While progress was made during the early production runs, the final result still was not satisfactory. This problem had never been an issue in the past because the day fighter types were not affected. Now that the Air Corps was in urgent need of

a night fighter, it became a glaring issue. If an enemy aircraft had a gunner or rear facing observer on-board, the flame from the exhaust would be a dead giveaway. Even if the enemy only had a pilot, should the P-61 come in behind too fast and overshoot, then it would be easy for the enemy to fire at the Black Widow.

Another weakness that was pointed out by the operational pilots in the field, was the P-61's lack of range. This criticism was addressed by adding external wing racks on the wings, thus allowing 310-gallon fuel tanks to be attached. When you hung four of these on the aircraft,

the range extended considerably.

The only competitor that the Black Widow had within the Air Corp's inventory was the converted A-20 Havoc, known as the P-70. The personalities of both aircraft were similar in some areas and poles apart in others. The P-61 was about 10,000 pounds heavier, five feet longer and much more maneuverable and stable in flight. In speed, the P-61 was faster at all altitudes, especially above 15,000 feet. They were closely matched in range and endurance. Without a doubt, once the Black Widow got into combat, she was hard to see, hard to hit and hard to beat.

OPERATIONAL TEST & EVALUATION

ARMY AIR CORPS TEST PILOTS IRON OUT THE WRINKLES

The concept of the P-61 was sound and the design was exactly what the Army Air Force was looking for, but extensive tests still were to be conducted on the airframe to see exactly what it could do. Although the United States was engulfed in a world war and time was extremely important, the thoroughness of the test and evaluation was not compromised at all. Every facet of the Widow's personality and equipment was examined. When the final reports were released, every major and minor flaw was written up, with suggestions for changes. These were broken down into three sections, with top priority being given to items that required immediate attention, next would be a list of changes that were considered secondary, but would improve the aircraft's suitability as a night fighter.

Lastly, a list of modifications that would increase the P-61's combat efficiency.

These tests were carried out at Eglin Field, Florida, at the AAF Proving Grounds during the spring of 1944, and the final report was submitted on June 20. This final report showed several weaknesses in the P-61A models, but allowed that some of these problems could be eliminated with the addition of the big water-injection R-2800 C engines, which had a turbo supercharger. In other words, the P-61As were slightly underpowered. As stated in the report: "The performance of the A model falls off rapidly above its critical altitude of 21,000 feet." The lack of power needed to pursue an enemy aircraft at higher altitudes was the only prominent fault in the early models.

Further scrutiny of the report indicates: "The R-2800-10 powerplant reaches its critical altitude at about 22,000 feet. Above this, both power and performance drop quickly. If water injection were installed, higher power ratings could be used below the present military power, high blower critical altitude. Previous tests of water injection on other type aircraft indicate that because engine operation is close to lean best power, performance is increased for some distance above critical altitude, although no manifold pressure increase is evidenced."

Altitude was one of the major issues discussed when the P-61 was developed. By the time this report was written up, it was common knowledge that the Japanese night bombers carried out their missions at approximately 25,000 feet. This

When it came to testing the P-61 Black Widow, these four test pilots were the heavyweights. Left to right are John W. Myers, Max R. Stanley, Harry Crosby and Alex Papana. Myers went into the forward areas in the Southwest Pacific and showed the young pilots how to get the maximum out of the big fighter. He gave the pilots a tremendous amount of confidence in the new night fighter, many of them still talk about his demonstrations even today. (Northrop)

WARBIRDTECH
S E R I E S

This YP-61 is undergoing landing gear emergency release test. At this point the YP models were in the early stages of their test and evaluation. Note the Northrop officials and military personnel present for the test. (Roy Wolford)

This is one of the most unusual photographs taken during the YP-61 flight testing. Note the translucent nose that exposes the features of the highly classified radar. More than likely, this aircraft was operating from a very secure area, away from cameras. (Castle Graphics)

An in-flight close up of the seventh production YP-61. This particular aircraft was widely photographed by the media, and the painting on the side of the nose depicting a black widow spider and her web was for publicity purposes. (Roy Wolford)

knowledge was provided by the P-70 pilots who were intercepting these bombers, in the Pacific. The underpowered P-70 would all but be hanging on its props and still not be high enough to make the kill.

Final conclusions drawn by the test team during its testing of the YP-61 Black Widow's potential night fighter role were:

1. Lack of sufficient gas supply for required lengthy night patrols.

2. Poor location and difficult operation of engine cooling control switches and levers.

3. Exhaust flare not adequately dampened.

4. Excessive length of time necessary to load guns.

5. At slow gliding speeds, there is a small dead spot in the aileron control in which there is no aileron response. Aileron control at low speeds is inadequate when taking off in propeller wash or crosswinds.

6. Unreliable induction system which produces large differences in available power in successive flights.

7. The forces on aileron and elevator control are excessive at high speeds.

8. Dense smoke and fumes enter both fore and aft crew compartments when the 20MM cannon are fired.

9. Trim tab controls all move in a vertical plane and do not have a clearly denoted neutral reference point.

10. The P-61 is unable to dive over 350 MPH indicated airspeed without use of excessive forward pressure on the control column.

11. Gun flash from the top turret detracts from the night vision of both the pilot and gunner.

12. Lack of adequate heating and poor cockpit sealing.

13. The remote indicating compass, Type AN5730-2, is not adequate.

14. Lack of tail warning device.

The above 14 items were considered to be major problems and steps must be taken to correct them. Fifteen minor objections were also noted in the report. They showed just how thorough and detailed the tests were:

One of the early P-61A models gets some last minute attention prior to another test flight. The Dash-5 began with the forty-sixth P-61 produced. The 2,250 horsepower engines replaced the 2,000HP engine in this series. Both squadrons that operated the Black Widow out of England in 1944 (422nd and 425th NFS) flew the Dash -5s. (Northrop)

1. Carburetor pre-heat door hinges are unsatisfactory.

2. Manifold pressure regulators were not set properly at the factory.

3. The directional instability of two YP-61s delivered to this test center had to be corrected by a makeshift rudder modification sent out by the factory.

4. Pilot's trap door is not jettisonable.

5. Forward visibility in the rain is poor and the present clear vision panels obstruct normal vision.

6. Turn and bank indicator is not mounted in the center of the instrument panel.

7. Brake hydraulic lines run too close to the main landing wheels.

8. The present type throttle quadrant is not satisfactory.

9. Long hydraulic pump handle interferes with radio operation.

10. Starter and primer switches are difficult to reach.

11. Battery switches too numerous.

12. The automatic pilot does not warrant the large portion of the control panel it occupies.

13. The many formers of the canopy obstruct the pilot's visibility.

14. A speaking tube from the pilot to radar operator is required in case of interphone failure.

15. Some means of rapid deceleration is required on a night fighter.

After all testing was completed, the evaluation team presented the following four modifications that were to be acted on immediately:

1. Remove the present engine and replace it with a C-type water injection R-2800-22W engine. If this was not possible, then install a B type water injection R-2800-LOW.

2. Every effort be made to decrease weight and increase power so that additional speed can be obtained. Experiments with paddle blade propellers in an attempt to increase performance at altitude and in climb.

3. Install and test a turbo supercharged engine on one aircraft in an effort to improve its performance at altitude.

4. The aircraft be made aerodynamically cleaner.

The following modifications were suggested to improve the operational suitability of the P-61A as a night fighter:

1. Make provisions to carry more internal fuel and provide external racks for carrying external fuel tanks.

2. All engine shutter and cowl flaps be automatically controlled.

Frontal view of an XP-61 being run-up on the ramp at the Northrop facility in Hawthorne, California. The first pilot to fly the XP was Vance Breese, a well-known test pilot in the aviation industry. (Gerald Balzer)

3. Develop new exhaust stacks that will more adequately damp the exhaust flare.

4. Study the armament installation to determine the possibility of reducing the amount of time needed to re-arm the aircraft.

5. Immediately correct the dead spot in the ailerons at slow speeds and the lack of positive aileron control at low speeds.

6. Check the induction system to discover the cause of large variation in power available on successive flights.

7. Try spring-loaded tabs (similar to those used on the Navy F6F Hellcat) or other means on the elevators and ailerons with a view toward reducing stick forces and providing more positive control at low speeds.

8. Take steps to prevent smoke and fumes from entering the cockpit when the guns are fired.

9. Trim tab controls should be the conventional fighter type with neutral position indicated, so as to be easily checked at night by feel.

10. Investigate the longitudinal trim and control surfaces to correct excessive nose up tendency in high-speed dives.

11. Investigate all possibilities for reducing the flash of the .50-caliber guns when fired. If a solution is found, it is recommended that it be put into effect immediately. The loss of night vision by the pilot and gunner in a combat situation could be disastrous.

12. A heater with more output at altitude will be necessary. Cockpit sealing definitely needs improvement, with particular attention given to improved design of the loose-fitting pilot's windows. They are very difficult to operate.

13. Install a type B-9 magnetic compass in addition to the remote indicating compass.

14. Install a taxiing light on the front of the nose wheel.

15. Incorporate a radar tail warning device in the aircraft.

The following modifications were suggested to increase the Black Widow's combat efficiency:

1. The hinges on the carburetor preheat doors should be reinforced or made of a stronger material.

2. Factory-set all manifold pressure regulators at the proper balance pressure to allow maximum power up to the critical altitude, since the resetting of these regulators in the field is labor-intense and requires unnecessary check flights.

3. Modify all P-61A aircraft that are directionally unstable before an attempt is made to fly them in instrument weather conditions.

4. The pilot's trap door should be jettisonable to provide an additional escape hatch.

WARBIRD**TECH**
S E R I E S

Northrop pilot Richard Ronaldi and crew chief Joe Burden discuss specific adjustments that were to necessary after a test flight out of the Northrop facility. This was an A model. (Gerald Balzer)

5. Add a fluid or film that will prevent the spotting condition that exists on bullet-resistant glass while flying through rain. The clear vision panels should not be installed in future aircraft as they decrease the necessary search view of the pilot.

6. Move the turn and bank indicator to a more central position on the instrument panel.

7. Move the brake hydraulic lines to clear the landing wheels by about 5 inches.

8. Install a fighter type throttle quadrant, similar to the one in the P-38 Lightning.

9. Hydraulic pump handle should be a telescopic type.

10. Move the starter and primer switches to a more readily accessible position on the instrument panel. (11)...All battery switches should be controlled by a drop bar type single lever.

12. Remove the automatic pilot and relocate the flight instruments to a more logical location.

13. A clear Plexiglas canopy would be a decided aid to the pilot.

14. Install an intercommunication tube from the radar operator to the pilot, allowing communication between the two in the event of interphone failure.

15. Design and test a deceleration flap in an endeavor to produce rapid deceleration.

Some of the test hops were used to provide good photo opportunities. This early P-61A model was caught by Northrop photographer Roy Wolford in flight over the mountainous terrain of California. Many of the pictures taken on this flight were used extensively by Northrop for publicity purposes. (Wolford)

ANATOMY OF THE P-61

If it were possible to disassemble a Black Widow and look at each part, you would understand just what an engineering marvel it was. It never ceases to amaze me how gifted John Northrop and his team of aeronautical engineers were. They satisfied a desperate need in a very short span of time and any flaws that the Black Widow had were easily corrected. Neither the Germans nor the Japanese were able to put anything up that could answer the Spider's sting.

The dimensions of the P-61 are:

Wing Span = 66 feet

Overall Length = 49 feet, 7 inches

Height = 14 feet, 8 inches

Height to Propeller Hubs = 7 feet

Dihedral of the Outer Wing = 2 degrees

Dihedral of the Inner Wing = 4 degrees

The wing structure is divided into seven sections: two wing tips of welded magnesium alloy, two outer panels, two inner wing panels, and the spar sections (front and rear) that extend through the crew nacelle.

Looking down the long aft segment of the engine nacelle in the XP-61, note the installation of the oxygen bottles and the control cables leading to the vertical and horizontal stabilizers. Three oxygen regulators located at the side of each crew station above the right cockpit rail could supply the correct mixture of air and oxygen required at any altitude. (Northrop)

WARBIRDTECH SERIES

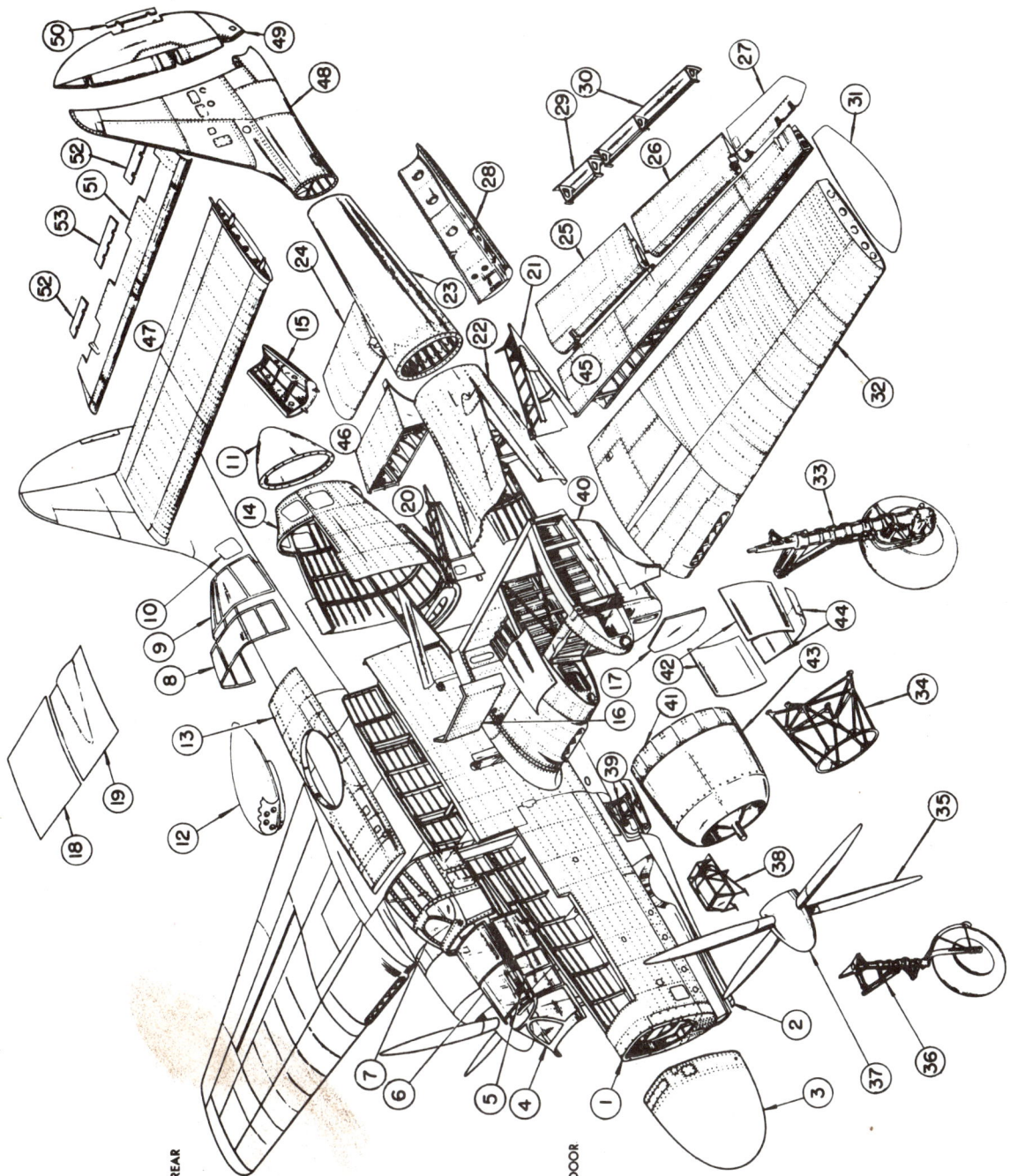

1. CREW NACELLE FORWARD AND INTERMEDIATE SECTIONS
2. DOOR ASSEMBLY – NOSE WHEEL
3. NOSE ASSEMBLY – CREW NACELLE
4. PILOT'S WINDSHIELD
5. PILOT'S ENCLOSURE PANEL
6. PILOT'S HINGED CANOPY
7. GUNNER'S ENCLOSURE
8. ENCLOSURE – REAR HINGED
9. ENCLOSURE – REAR FIXED
10. RADIO OPERATOR'S WINDOWS
11. CONE ASSEMBLY – CREW NACELLE REAR
12. ELECTRICAL GUN TURRET
13. CREW NACELLE TURRET ASSEMBLY
14. CREW NACELLE AFT SECTION
15. RADIO OPERATOR'S DOOR
16. INNER WING TANK PANEL
17. ENGINE NACELLE – FORWARD LOWER PANEL
18. COVER ASSEMBLY INBOARD
19. COVER – INNER WING FUEL TANK
20. STUB WING INBOARD
21. STUB WING OUTBOARD
22. ENGINE NACELLE
23. TAIL BOOM ASSEMBLY
24. INNER WING FLAP ASSEMBLY
25. OUTER WING FLAP INBOARD
26. OUTER WING FLAP OUTBOARD
27. AILERON ASSEMBLY
28. MAIN LANDING GEAR DOOR
29. SPOILER INBOARD
30. SPOILER OUTBOARD
31. WING TIP
32. OUTER WING MAIN SECTION
33. MAIN LANDING GEAR
34. ENGINE MOUNT
35. PROPELLER ASSEMBLY
36. NOSE LANDING GEAR
37. SPINNER ASSEMBLY
38. CREW NACELLE FRONT ENTRANCE DOOR
39. CANNON COVER
40. INNER WING MAIN SECTION
41. FLAP ASSEMBLY
42. PANEL ASSEMBLY
43. COWL PANEL
44. COWL ACCESS FLAP
45. OUTER WING TRAILING SECTION
46. INNER WING
47. TRAILING SECTION PANEL
48. HORIZONTAL STABILIZER
49. VERTICAL STABILIZER
50. RUDDER ASSEMBLY
51. RUDDER TAB
52. ELEVATOR ASSEMBLY
53. SERVO TAB
53. ELEVATOR TRIM TAB

This cutaway shows all of the major parts that fit together to form the greatest night fighter/all-weather fighter to emerge from World War II. It is amazing that the Northrop engineers, in the short amount of time they had to do it, could put something this complicated together.

A look into the nose wheel compartment while the gear is down and locked. Early on, there were some problems with this area due to the lack of room when the wheel was up. You can see what damage would have been done if some of the tubing and cables had become crushed by the gear. (Roy Wolford)

The spars of the inner wing are not continuous through the centerline of the P-61, but are bolted to the spars in the crew nacelle at the top and bottom of each spar.

The complete wing assembly, except for the wing tips, is fully cantilevered,, riveted-aluminum-alloy, stressed-skin construction with the loads concentrated on the two main spars. The wing skin carries the chord bending and torsional loads and is supported by chordwise ribs and stiffeners, plus such spanwise stiffeners as are necessary to prevent skin wrinkling. Even the later C models showed a limited amount of wrinkling, so you can only imagine the amount of stress the area was subjected to.

Each inner wing panel contains an engine nacelle, two fuel tanks and a section of the wing flaps. They are built in two sections: the main section, which included the two spars, and the detachable trailing edge section, which includes the inboard flap.

The outer wing panels were bolted

A view of the right rear area of the Pratt & Whitney R-2800-10 two-stage, two-speed supercharged P-61 engine, designed to operate on 100-octane fuel. This particular powerplant is for the port side of the P-61. (Northrop)

to the inner wings at the top and bottom of each spar, and an oil tank and cooler were installed in each panel. The outer wing also was built in two sections: the main section, containing the two spars, and the detachable trailing edge section, which included wing flaps, spoiler panels and ailerons.

Six aluminum-alloy, hydraulically operated flaps of the slotted type are mounted on the trailing edges of the wings—two on each outer panel and one on each inner panel. All are linked so as to move aft and down when extended. It is noted that full flap deflection was 60 degrees, which is the key to the extremely slow landing speeds that are unique to the Black Widow.

In the extended position, there was a gap between the leading edge of the wing that permits a flow of air from the lower surface of the wing to the upper part of the flap. This smoothes the air flow over the flap and increases its lift at slow speeds and high angles of attack.

Retractable ailerons, resembling spoiler panels, are installed in the outer wings. They connect with small conventional ailerons at the wing tips, which serve only to give "feel" to the aileron operation. Because of the full-span landing flaps, which run almost the entire length of the outer wing panels, the ailerons are necessarily small in area.

The retractable ailerons are curved panels of perforated metal. In the neutral position they retract within the outer wing panel near the trailing

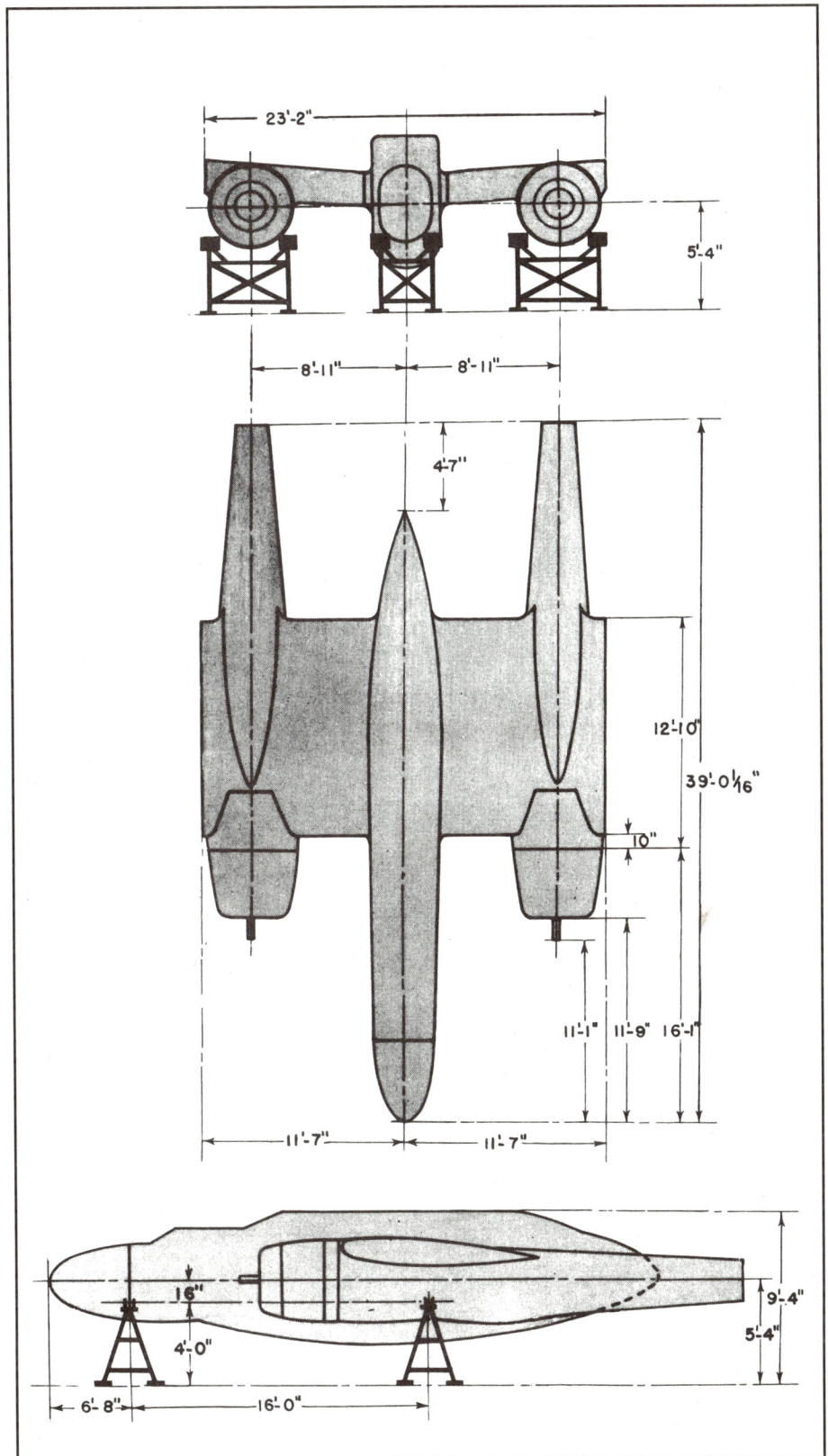

None of the P-61s had the range to make the flight from the United States to Hawaii or Europe. Most were carefully crated and shipped on the decks of Navy ships. The crating procedure was complicated and numerous man hours were required to prepare one aircraft for shipment overseas.

through the center of the nacelle in front of and behind the gun turret.

The nose section forward of the pilot's compartment is built of resin-impregnated fiberglass. It encloses the spinner and other units of the radar section equipment. This section is attached to the crew nacelle by four locating studs and four toggle latches.

Positioned directly behind the pilot is the gunner's station and connected by an access door are the pilot's and gunner's enclosure, which is made of molded Lucite sheets bound by extruded aluminum alloy frames. The section directly over the gunner is supported by square steel tubing. A hinged window on each side is provided for the pilot. An access panel is located over the pilot's seat, and an emergency kick-out panel to the right of the gunner's seat can be opened from inside or out. These would only be used in emergency situations in cases when the aircraft had bellied in on the ground or ditched in the water.

The flexible gun turret with four .50-caliber machine guns is mounted between the two wing spars and protrudes through the top of the crew nacelle. From a side angle or a three-quarter frontal view, it was this black turret that gave the P-61 such an ominous appearance.

The radar operator's position in the aft portion of the crew nacelle is totally separated from the pilot and

edge, inboard of the ailerons. Later models of the Black Widow, such as the C and D models, are equipped with fighter brakes—slotted panels that create high drag and slow the aircraft rapidly without making it veer off course. These were used when the fighter was closing too fast, allowing the pilot to correct, yet still keep the enemy aircraft in his sights.

On the early models, a combination trim and booster tab, controllable manually from the cockpit, was fitted to the left aileron. A booster tab fitted to the right aileron was adjustable on the ground only. The ailerons of later models are not equipped with these tabs.

The crew nacelle contains the pilot's cockpit and stations for the gunner and the radar operator. Its main structural members are transverse channel-type frames; longitudinal, extruded-aluminum-alloy bulb angles; and the stressed skin. Special stiffeners distribute concentrated stresses at the cockpit enclosures, gun turret, nose wheel well and entrance door cutouts. The wing front and rear spars are bolted to spar extensions, which pass

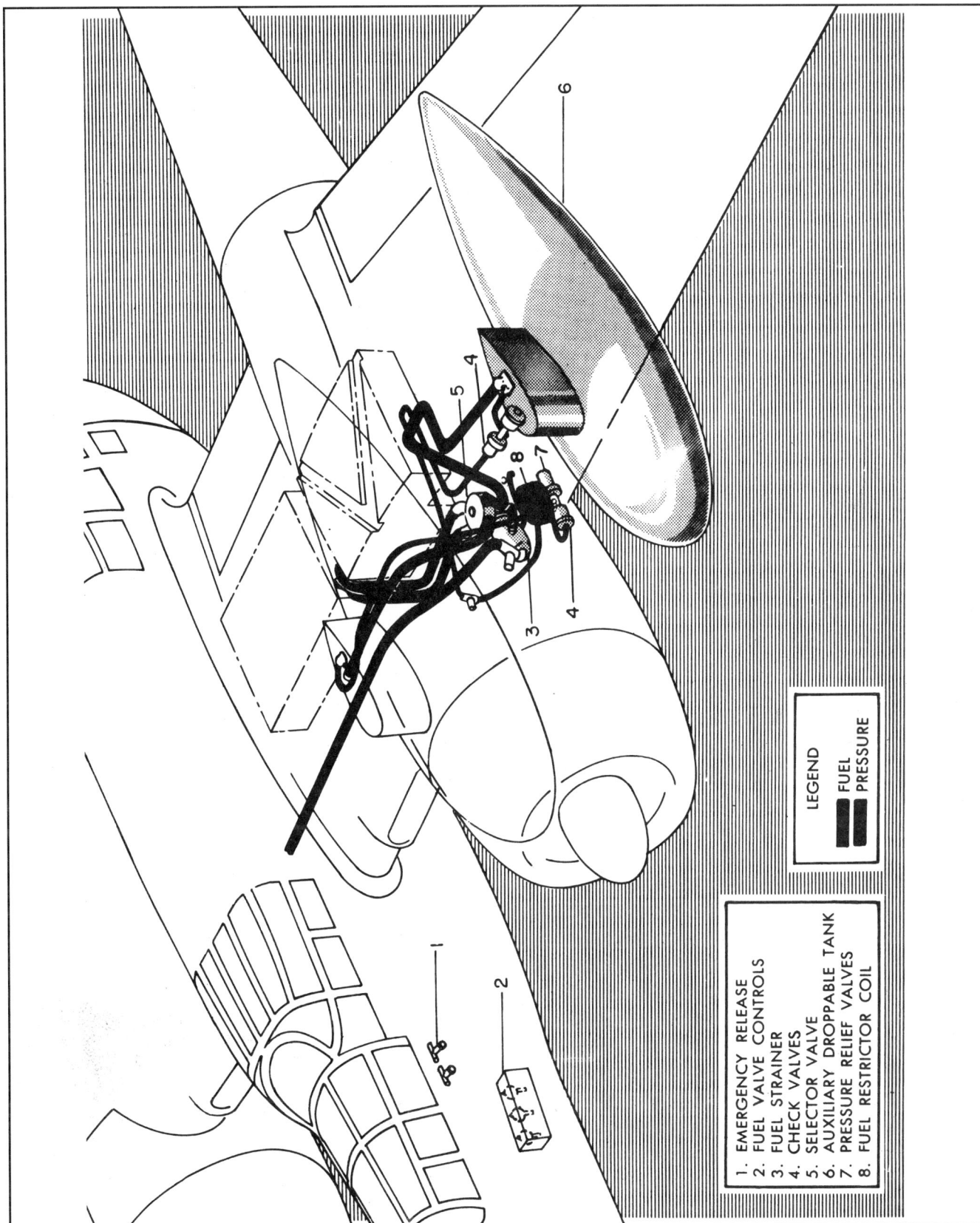

LEGEND

FUEL
PRESSURE

1. EMERGENCY RELEASE
2. FUEL VALVE CONTROLS
3. FUEL STRAINER
4. CHECK VALVES
5. SELECTOR VALVE
6. AUXILIARY DROPPABLE TANK
7. PRESSURE RELIEF VALVES
8. FUEL RESTRICTOR COIL

This diagram shows the intricate fuel line system that had the variable-speed. electric-motor-driven booster pump as its focal point. These pumps (right and left wings) were all interconnected and capable of transferring fuel in a number of combinations. This shows the system with all four droppable fuel tanks (310 gallons each) included.

The main tires on the Black Widow were 47.0-inch smooth contour types that were manufactured by Goodyear. Tire pressure is set at 40 PSI. (Northrop)

gunner's compartment by the gun turret and all of the radio equipment. Because of this separation, the test teams had suggested that a tube be installed to enable the radar operator to talk to the pilot if the interphone failed. In a critical situation, the pilot might be preparing to bail out and the crew member in the rear would be unaware of it. The radar operator's compartment is formed of molded Lucite sheets bound with extruded aluminum frames. The tail cone is made of two molded sheets of Lucite cemented together at the vertical centerline and bolted to the aftermost frame of the crew nacelle.

The pilot's and gunner's entrance door, located just aft of the pilot's seat, is combined with the nose wheel well. The door frame and folding ladder formed a welded steel structure that is hinged at the forward end. The aluminum alloy wheel well is riveted to the door structure.

The two tail booms extend aft from the engine nacelles to the vertical stabilizer assemblies. The booms are made of monocoque construc-

The rear cone on the crew nacelle is made of two molded sheets of Lucite that have been cemented together at the vertical centerline and bolted to the aftermost frame of the crew nacelle. Black Widow ace Herman Ernst had the tail cone in his P-61 disintegrate on him while he was diving on a German V-1 Buzz Bomb. (Northrop)

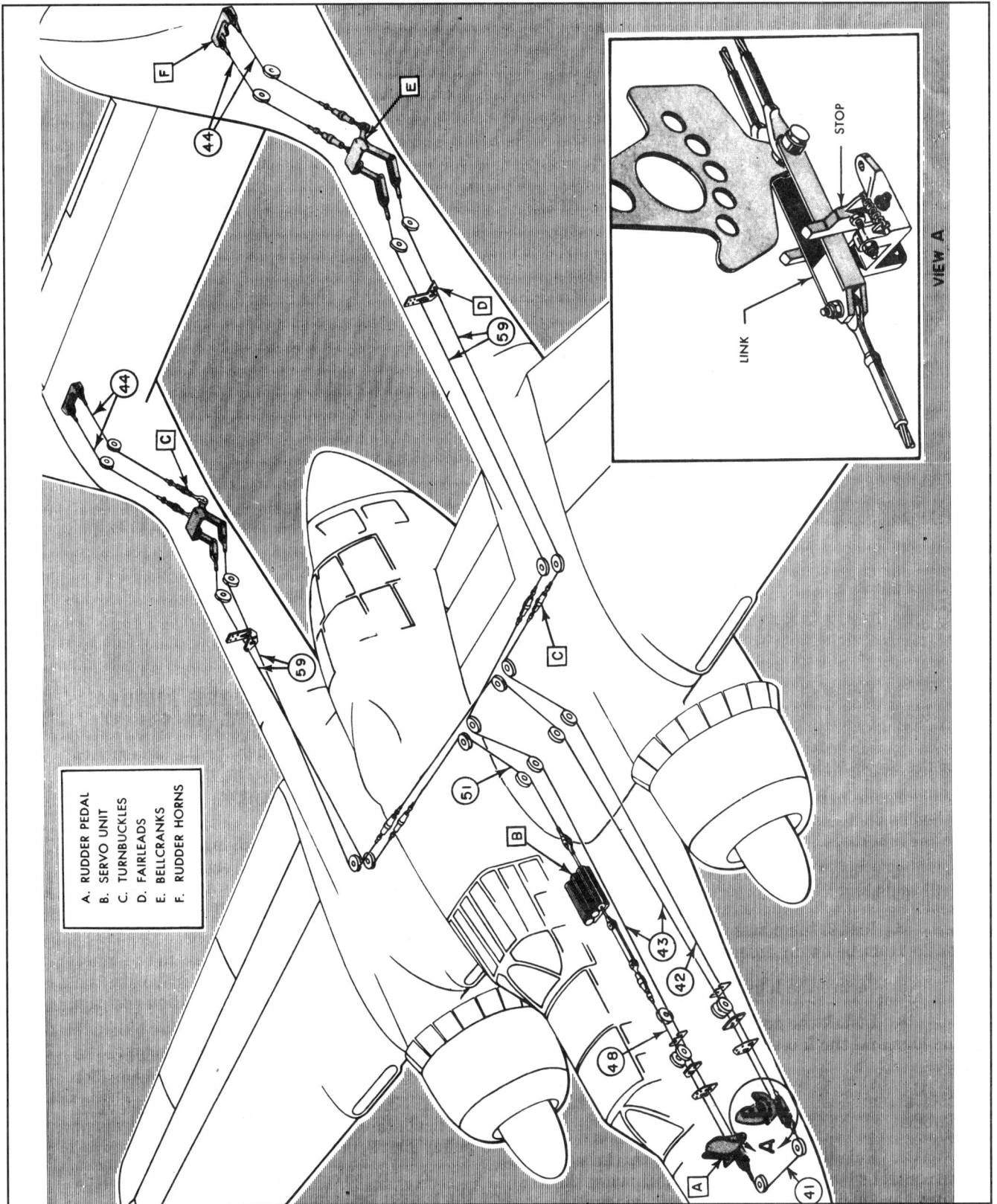

VIEW A

STOP

LINK

A. RUDDER PEDAL
B. SERVO UNIT
C. TURNBUCKLES
D. FAIRLEADS
E. BELLCRANKS
F. RUDDER HORNS

On separate occasions, the P-61 was required to prove itself against the P-47 and the Beaufighter. It came out on top in both encounters, and one of the reasons was its outstanding maneuverability. This drawing shows the rudder control system that allows the aircraft such distinct turning ability. The rudders are limited in movement to 25 degrees each side of the neutral position.

A one-quarter top rear view of the inner wing assembly on a P-61A shows six oxygen bottles aft of the wing section. (Northrop)

tion and consist of riveted aluminum alloy frames, stiffeners and skin. Bolts through forged steel brackets attach the boom structures to the empennage and engine nacelle sections. Communications and identification antennae and the remote indicating compass transmitter are housed in the booms.

The empennage includes the horizontal stabilizer structure and elevator, two vertical stabilizers, which are faired into the tail booms, and two rudders. The horizontal and vertical stabilizers are of all-metal construction. Two spanwise spars support the horizontal stabilizer structure and the contour is formed by aluminum alloy ribs and skin. It bolts to the vertical stabilizers at the ends of the spars and is faired with light, removable fairing strips.

The closing channel at the trailing edge forms the main spar of the vertical stabilizer. An auxiliary spar located just aft of the leading edge of the stabilizer extends down from the tip for approximately 6 feet. The lower portion of each vertical stabilizer forms the aft end of one of the tail booms and each attaches to the boom by an elliptical internal attaching angle.

The elevators and rudders are constructed of fabric-covered aluminum alloy, and each is statically

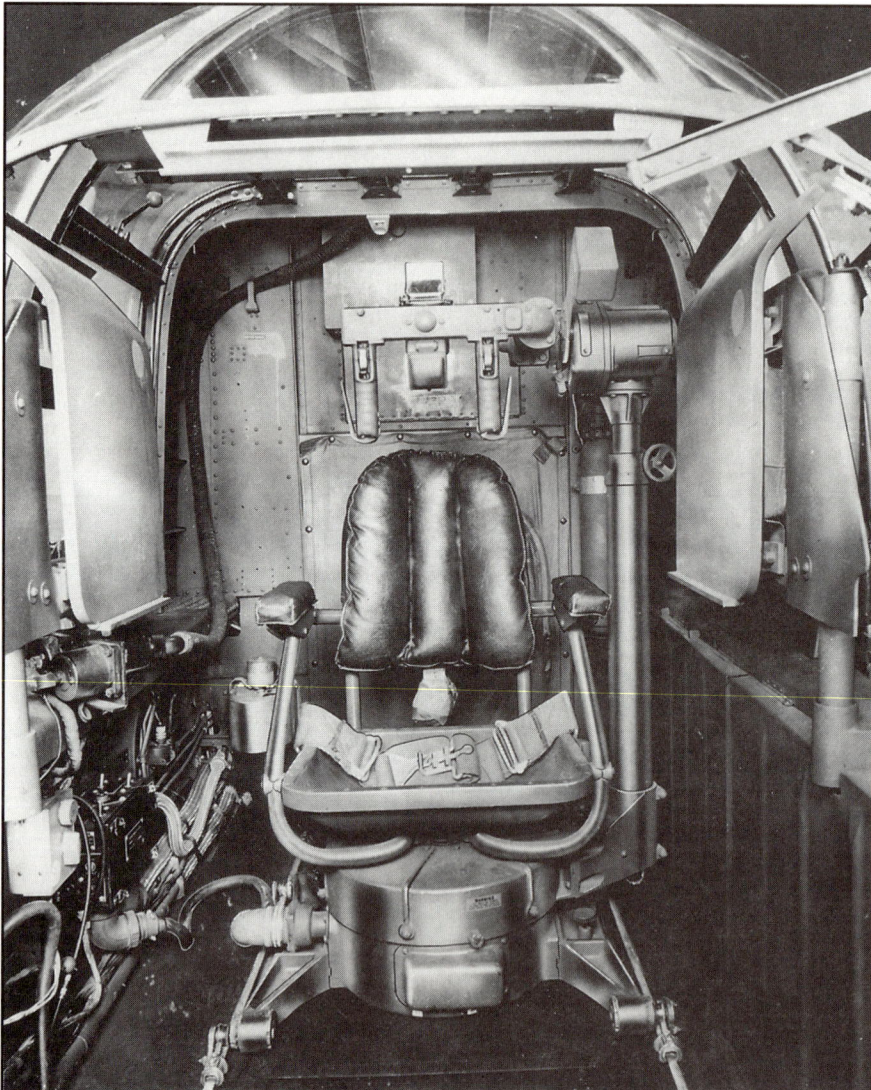

A frontal view of the gunner's compartment shows everything in the combat ready position. The sighting device is secured in its operational mode. In most of the kills made from the P-61, the approach was from behind and slightly low, which required the upper turret guns to be elevated somewhat. (Northrop)

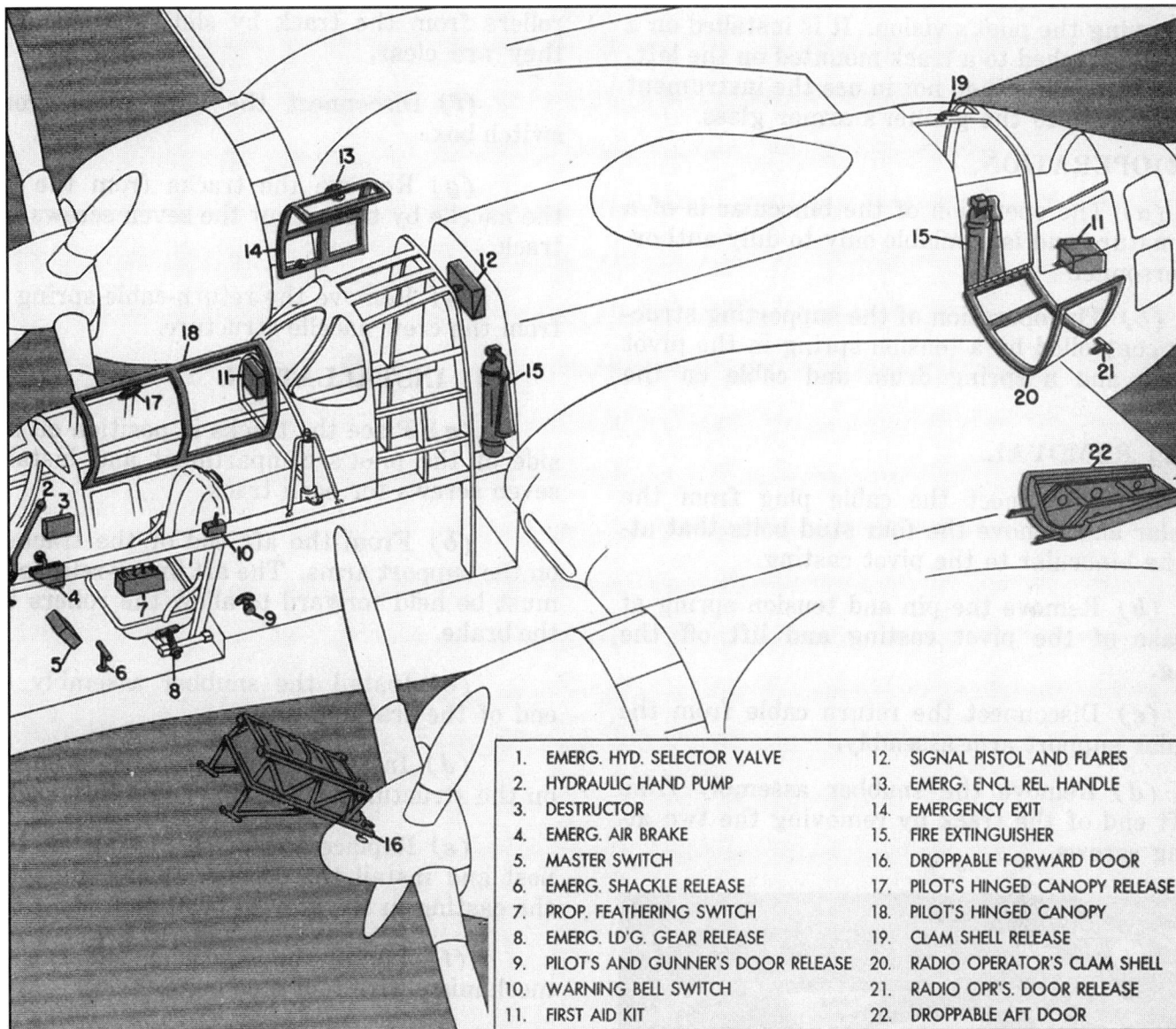

1.	EMERG. HYD. SELECTOR VALVE	12.	SIGNAL PISTOL AND FLARES
2.	HYDRAULIC HAND PUMP	13.	EMERG. ENCL. REL. HANDLE
3.	DESTRUCTOR	14.	EMERGENCY EXIT
4.	EMERG. AIR BRAKE	15.	FIRE EXTINGUISHER
5.	MASTER SWITCH	16.	DROPPABLE FORWARD DOOR
6.	EMERG. SHACKLE RELEASE	17.	PILOT'S HINGED CANOPY RELEASE
7.	PROP. FEATHERING SWITCH	18.	PILOT'S HINGED CANOPY
8.	EMERG. LD'G. GEAR RELEASE	19.	CLAM SHELL RELEASE
9.	PILOT'S AND GUNNER'S DOOR RELEASE	20.	RADIO OPERATOR'S CLAM SHELL
10.	WARNING BELL SWITCH	21.	RADIO OPR'S. DOOR RELEASE
11.	FIRST AID KIT	22.	DROPPABLE AFT DOOR

Each of the three crew positions in the P-61 provide two exits for each crew member. In the case of a bailout at a safe altitude, all members exit through the bottom of the aircraft. In the water or on the ground, all exit through the top or side of the aircraft.

and dynamically balanced. All-metal combination trim and booster tabs, controllable from the pilot's cockpit, are built into the trailing edge of the rudders. A combination trim and de-booster tab, also controllable from the pilot's cockpit, and two all-metal pre-loaded spring tabs, which are self-operating at high speeds to provide boost and reduce control forces, were built into the trailing edge of the elevator.

The fuel system of the P-61 provides a total of 646 gallons of fuel carried in four self-sealing tanks. A tank is located in each engine nacelle between the wing spars in each inner wing. The main nacelle tanks have a capacity of 205 gallons each, and the wing tanks each hold 118 gallons. The right hand wing tank is designated as reserve. A cross-feed line allows fuel from any tank to be made available to one or both engines. If you take

into consideration the four external, jettisonable 310-gallon fuel tanks that were added, the Black Widow had a potential capacity of close to 1,900 gallons on missions of long duration.

The tanks fit the contour of the wing structure on all sides and were attached at all tank outlet fittings. The top of each nacelle tank is laced to the V brace between front and rear wing spars. Each fuel tank contains a Thompson variable-speed electric fuel booster pump that is individually controlled and transfers fuel between the tanks at any altitude. They also supply fuel to engine-driven pumps under 6 to 8 PSI pressure to prevent vapor lock. A Type G-9 engine driven fuel pump of the rotary-vane, positive displacement type is mounted on each engine.

The Black Widow's hydraulic system operates the landing gear, main

503-022 NORTHROP
P-61 RUDDER FRAME ASSEM.

(Above) Good cutaway view showing the rudder. The elevator and rudders were constructed of fabric-covered aluminum alloy. The vertical stabilizers were of all-metal construction. (Northrop)

A three-quarter frontal view of the all-metal vertical stabilizer on an XP-61 with all of its service panels removed. The lower portion of each vertical stabilizer forms the aft end of the tail boom and is attached to the boom by an elliptical, internal attaching angle. (Northrop)

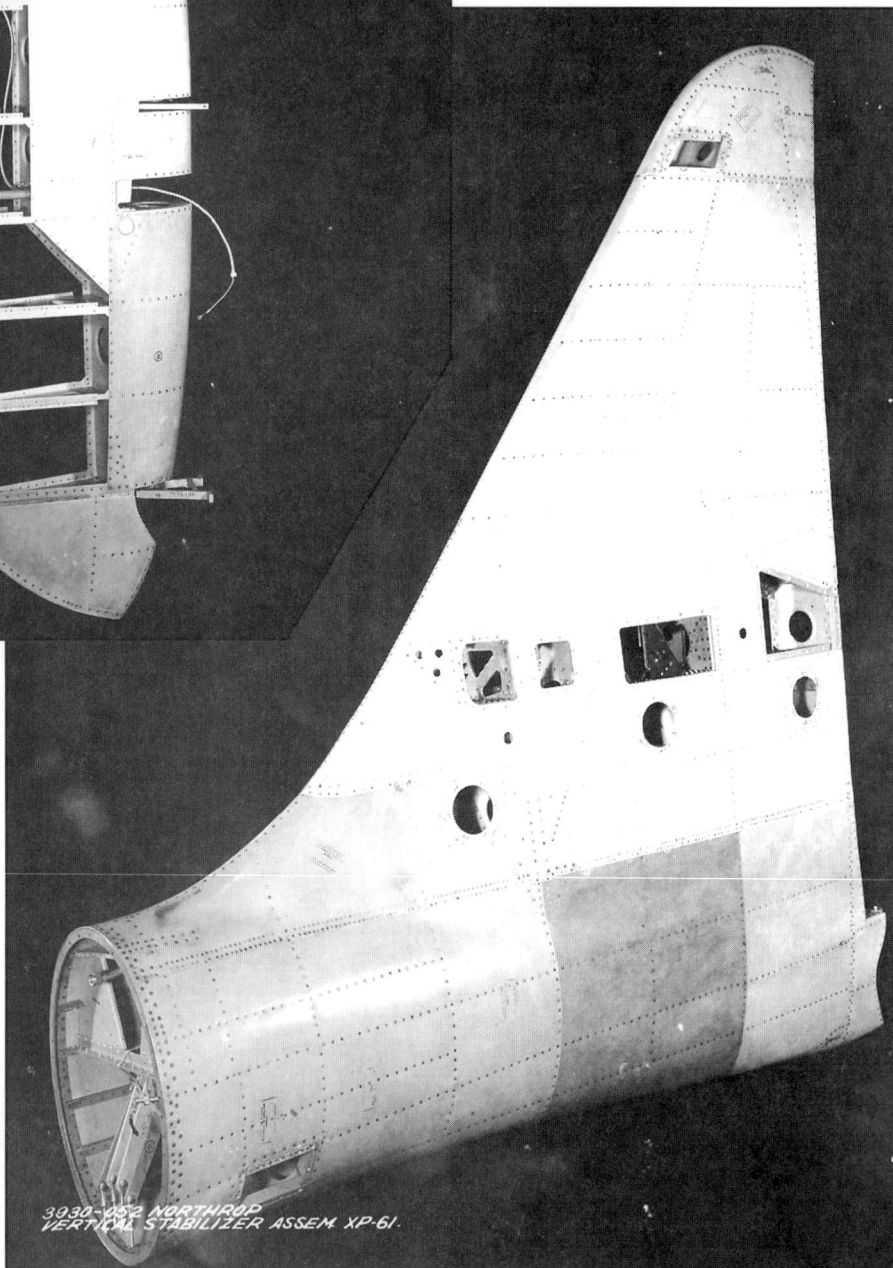

3930-052 NORTHROP
VERTICAL STABILIZER ASSEM XP-61.

WARBIRDTECH
SERIES

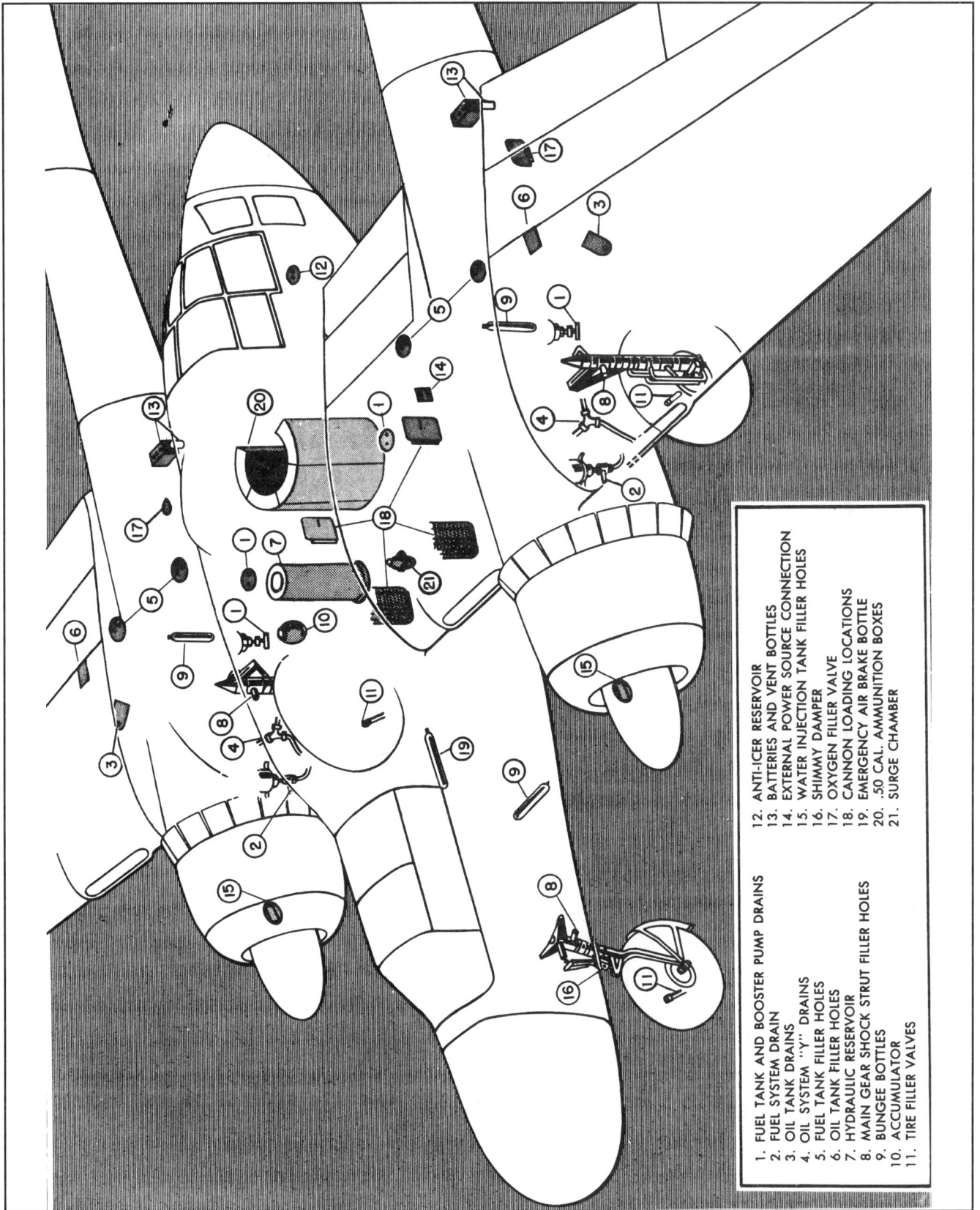

1. FUEL TANK AND BOOSTER PUMP DRAINS
2. FUEL SYSTEM DRAIN
3. OIL TANK DRAINS
4. OIL SYSTEM "Y" DRAINS
5. FUEL TANK FILLER HOLES
6. OIL TANK FILLER HOLES
7. HYDRAULIC RESERVOIR
8. MAIN GEAR SHOCK STRUT FILLER HOLES
9. BUNGEE BOTTLES
10. ACCUMULATOR
11. TIRE FILLER VALVES

12. ANTI-ICER RESERVOIR
13. BATTERIES AND VENT BOTTLES
14. EXTERNAL POWER SOURCE CONNECTION
15. WATER INJECTION TANK FILLER HOLES
16. SHIMMY DAMPER
17. OXYGEN FILLER VALVE
18. CANNON LOADING LOCATIONS
19. EMERGENCY AIR BRAKE BOTTLE
20. .50 CAL. AMMUNITION BOXES
21. SURGE CHAMBER

When you see a picture of the P-61 ground crews busy at work, this service diagram shows what they are doing. The 21 items mentioned on this page are vital to the performance and safety of the Black Widow. All of these require daily checks when the aircraft is flying on a regular basis.

NORTHROP
P-61 BLACK WIDOW

A visual demonstration of how to exit the gunner's compartment in an emergency situation that required parachuting out of the aircraft. (Gerald Balzer)

gear up and down latches and wheel doors, upper and lower engine cowl flaps, carburetor air heat valves, intercooler exit flaps (on the earlier models that were not equipped with superchargers), carburetor air filter, oil cooler air outlet doors, wing flaps, ejection chute doors and automatic pilot. The four main subdivisions of the hydraulic system are the main, accumulator, emergency, and automatic pilot systems.

Pressure is maintained in the system by an engine-driven hydraulic pump mounted on each engine accessory drive case. Fluid under pressure from both pumps converges and flows through a filter into an unloading valve, which maintains 850 to 1,000 PSI pressure in the main and accumulator systems. The valve also supplies fluid through the automatic pilot pressure regulator to the automatic pilot and to the reservoir.

Mounted on a bulkhead aft of the gunner's position is the hydraulic reservoir, accumulator, main pressure regulator, surge chamber and other units of the system. In the main system, pressure from the unloading valve is transmitted through a check valve directly to a manifold from which the fluid flows

The horizontal stabilizer is constructed of aluminum alloy ribs and covering supported by two spanwise spars. It is bolted to the vertical stabilizers at the ends of the spars and faired with light, easily removable fairing strips. (Northrop)

WARBIRD**TECH**
SERIES

1. OIL CELL
2. OUTBOARD FUEL CELL
3. ANTI-ICING FLUID
4. INBOARD FUEL CELL
5. HYDRAULIC FLUID
6. WATER

NO STEP AREA

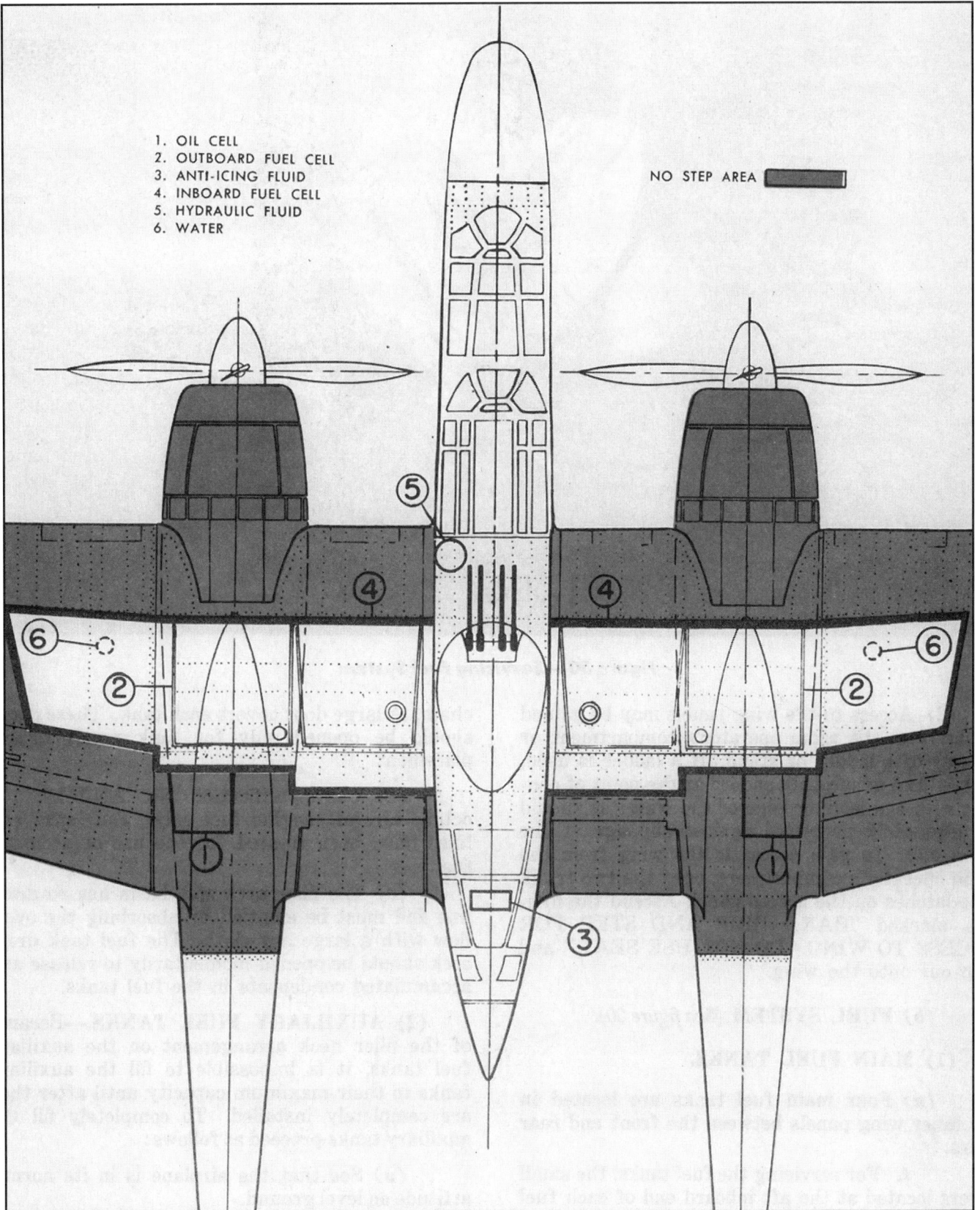

In the early P-61A models, the oil was carried in two 22-gallon self-sealing tanks located on each of the outer wing panels. In the later A models and in the P-61B, the capacity had increased to 42.5 gallons in two tanks and their position was shifted to one each in the engine nacelles.

One of the R-2800-10 powerplants, elevated by a hoist, is prepared to be placed into its engine nacelle on an XP-61 at the Northrop factory. (Gerald Balzer)

to the selector valves for landing gear, carburetor, air heat valves, oil cooler air outlet doors, engine cowl flaps and inter-cooler doors.

Hydraulic pressure from the accumulator system actuates the wing flaps, wheel brakes, ejection chute doors and the carburetor air filters. In the event of engine pump failure or of damage to the surge chamber or accumulator, all hydraulic units except the automatic pilot can be operated by the emergency system. By operating the hand pump of this system, fluid is forced to a selector valve from which it is directed to the main manifolds, the main system or the accumulator system.

The main pressure regulator is mounted on the aft edge of the reservoir support. This valve was permanently set to maintain a maximum of 1,000 PSI and a minimum of 850 PSI of pressure in the main and accumulator systems. At maximum pressure, fluid is directed to the automatic pilot pressure regulator.

The surge chamber in the main system is mounted below the reservoir, divided by a flexible diaphragm into two parts. The upper part is filled with the hydraulic fluid and is

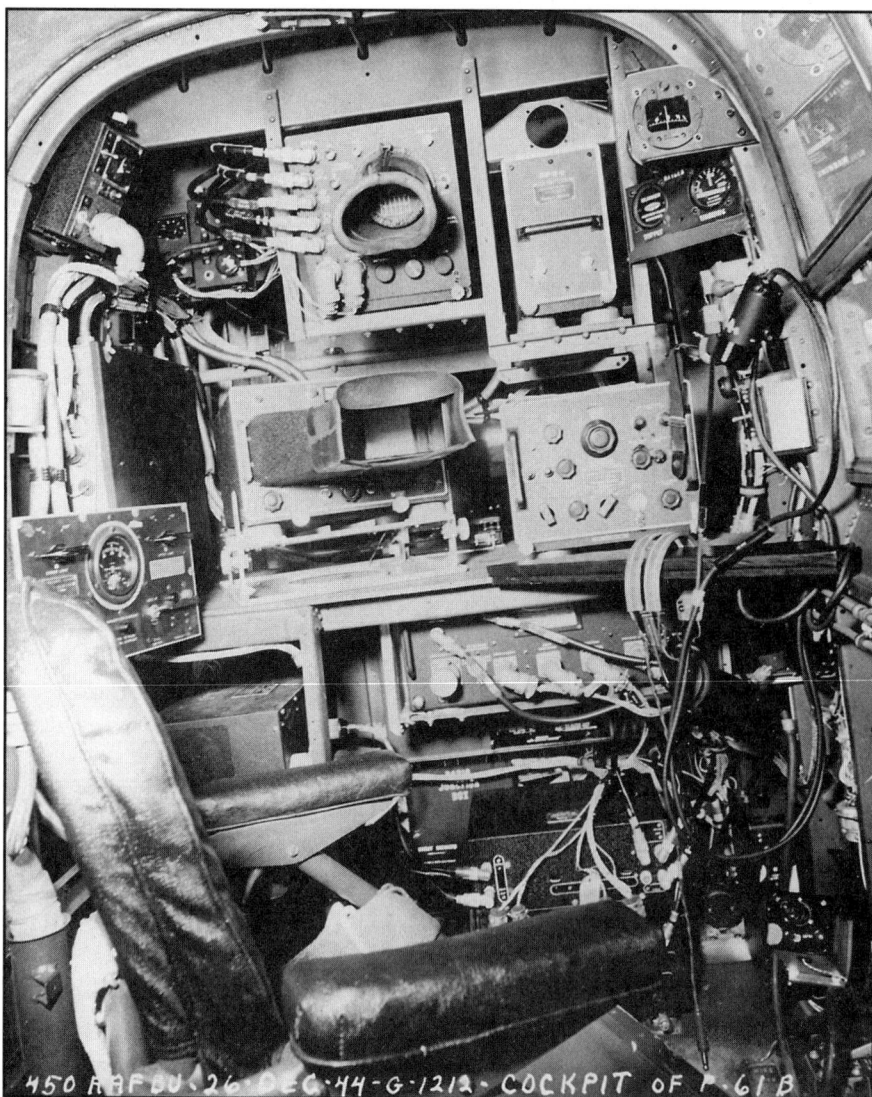

A view from the rear. This radar operator's compartment is fully loaded with gear and ready for combat. It appears to be almost as complicated as the pilot's cockpit. When the R/O is operating the equipment, he is facing toward the front of the aircraft. (Northrop)

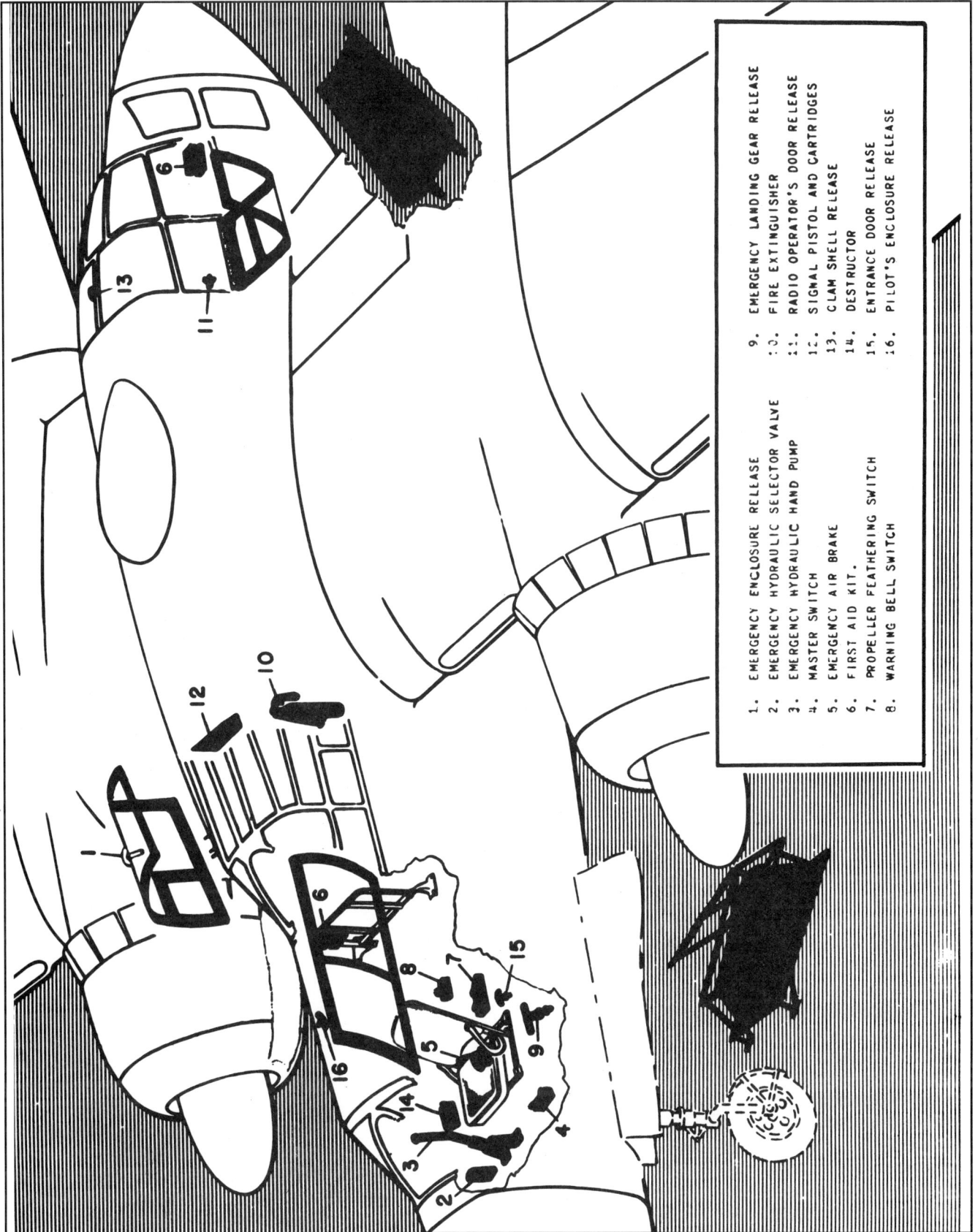

This cutaway diagram points out the exits and equipment to the crew members in an emergency situation. The top and side exits were only for exiting while the aircraft was on the ground. (Northrop)

1. EMERGENCY ENCLOSURE RELEASE
2. EMERGENCY HYDRAULIC SELECTOR VALVE
3. EMERGENCY HYDRAULIC HAND PUMP
4. MASTER SWITCH
5. EMERGENCY AIR BRAKE
6. FIRST AID KIT.
7. PROPELLER FEATHERING SWITCH
8. WARNING BELL SWITCH

9. EMERGENCY LANDING GEAR RELEASE
10. FIRE EXTINGUISHER
11. RADIO OPERATOR'S DOOR RELEASE
12. SIGNAL PISTOL AND CARTRIDGES
13. CLAM SHELL RELEASE
14. DESTRUCTOR
15. ENTRANCE DOOR RELEASE
16. PILOT'S ENCLOSURE RELEASE

A training accident as a result of nose gear failure has temporarily taken the first production YP-61 off the operational list. (AF Serial number 41-18876) was the first of thirteen YP models built by Northrop. This was taken in April 22, 1944, which was after the P-61A had gone operational with the Air Corps. (Northrop)

directly connected to the pressure line. The lower part contains compressed air, which forms a cushion and maintains a back pressure against the main pressure regulator valve that prevents it from constant functioning or pounding due to small changes in fluid volume.

Each engine nacelle is a semi-monocoque structure consisting of stressed skin, longitudinal stringers, and transverse frames. The loads applied directly to the engine mount, main alighting gear, fuel tank and tail boom are transferred to the basic wing structure through the structural strength of the

engine nacelle. This load transfer results in a highly stressed structure, both during flight and while landing.

The forward nacelle structure is made up of three sections: inboard, outboard and lower forward sections. The upper and lower ends are built as an integral part, respectively, of the bulkheads and keel structures on each side of the landing gear cutouts. The aft structure of the nacelle is attached directly to the forward structure by riveted keel and stringer splices and to the rear spar by two fittings. All stringers in the nacelle structure

are 24 ST extruded bulb angles. The nacelle frames are built up, formed single channel sections or double channel sections riveted back-to-back.

The P-61 is equipped with retractable, tricycle-type landing gear. The two units of the main gear extend from each engine nacelle, and the auxiliary nose gear extends from the crew nacelle. When retracted, the alighting gear is completely enclosed by doors, which when closed form the lower contour of the nacelles.

Each unit of the main landing gear

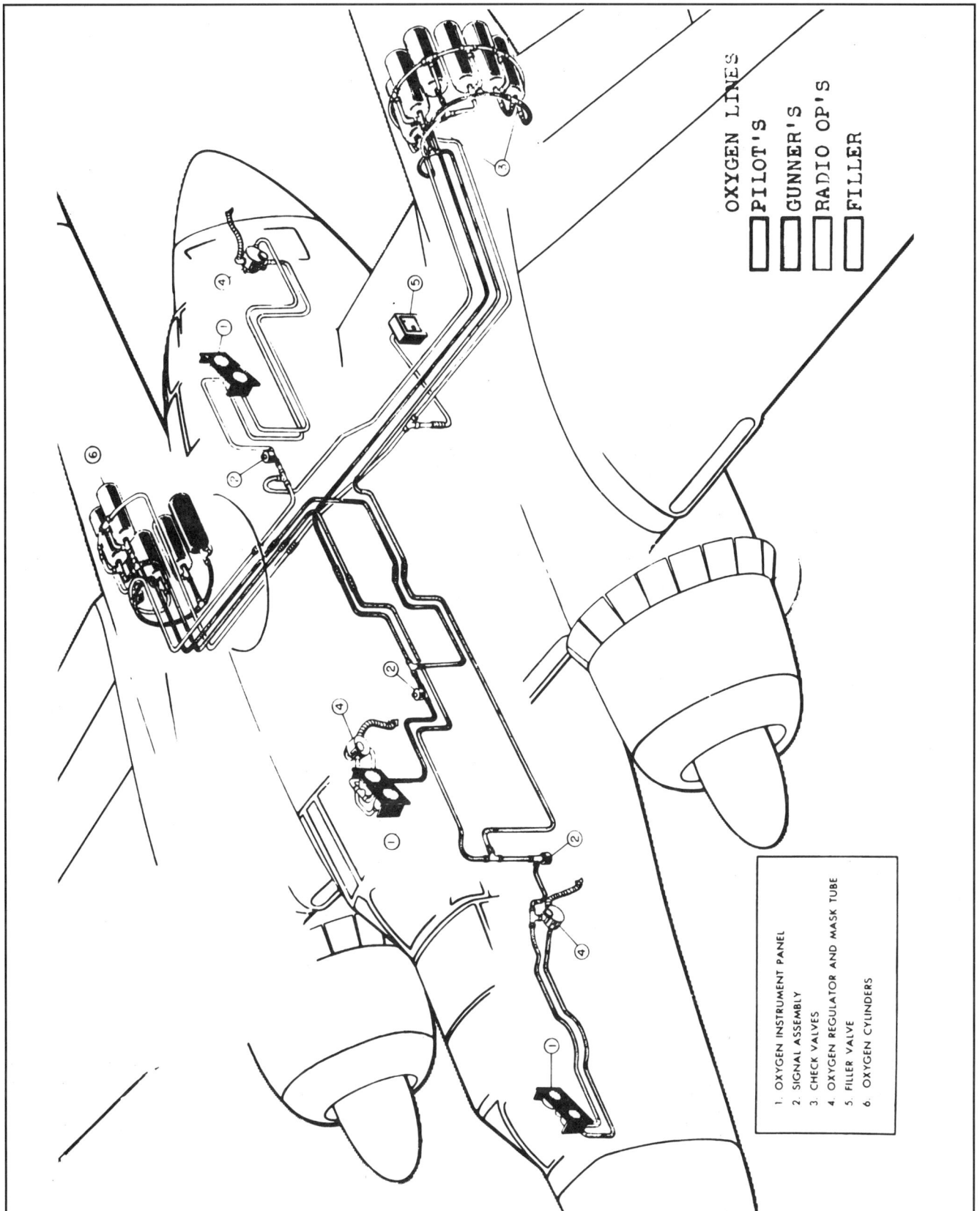

OXYGEN LINES

PILOT'S
GUNNER'S
RADIO OP'S
FILLER

1. OXYGEN INSTRUMENT PANEL
2. SIGNAL ASSEMBLY
3. CHECK VALVES
4. OXYGEN REGULATOR AND MASK TUBE
5. FILLER VALVE
6. OXYGEN CYLINDERS

A detailed schematic shows the oxygen supply lines coming from both storage areas to the three crew compartments. There were six cylinders neatly stowed in the rear area of each engine nacelle. The ground crews were instructed to check out this system before the aircrews arrived for a mission—it was a top priority. (Northrop)

An expanded view of a nose gear accident that happened while the aircraft was taxiing at the Northrop plant. This was YP-61 #18876. Note the Martin B-26 parked nearby, which was probably used in the night fighter training program as a TB-26. (Northrop)

is supported by two steel castings, which are bolted (one on each side of the nacelle) to closed box keel structures built into the nacelle on each side of the cutout that was provided to accommodate the retracted gear. Landing loads are transmitted through the shock strut to the side thrust brace, the two trunions, the downlock and the main supports.

The main gear retracting cylinder and uplock, and their fittings, are attached to a diaphragm or bulkhead structure installed transversely across the engine nacelle at the aft end of the cutout. The diaphragm reinforces the nacelle frame as well as supports the cylinder and uplock assemblies.

In retracting, the gear hinges on two trunion pins at the two steel castings. Both pins are secured by lock bolts. One end of the actuating cylinder is attached to the drag arm, or head, of the shock strut. A side thrust brace is mounted between the inboard end of the

trunion and the shock strut to absorb side loads.

The main gear is held in position when extended and retracted by mechanical latching mechanisms. If the gear fails to latch in the down position and the throttle is closed to less than 1,000 RPM, a warning horn sounds. An emergency system extends the gear in the event of hydraulic system failure.

The nose gear is supported by two brackets, one on each side of the crew nacelle, and hinges on trunion pins that pass through needle bearings and into the trunion structure. Both pins are secured in place by lock bolts. A folding drag link assembly also supports the gear when it is in the extended latched position.

A warning horn, similar to the one provided for the main gear, sounds when the nose gear is not latched down and the throttle closes to 1000 RPM. A micro-switch wired to the gear and flap position indicator

registers when the gear is latched down. The nose gear is equipped with a shimmy damper to prevent rapid wheel oscillations.

Ailerons, spoilers and elevator are controlled in the conventional manner by the torque tube control column in the cockpit. The torque tube is attached at the base of the column and extends completely across the cockpit. Four control lines, at the extreme ends of the tube, attach to the four elevator control cables.

Ailerons and spoilers are controlled by the wheel on the control column by an enclosed sprocket and chain attached to the cables. From the chain ends, cables run aft along the left and right walls of the cockpit and outboard through the wings to the spoiler quadrants and then to the aileron quadrants.

From the spoiler quadrants, adjustable push-pull rods connect to differential bellcranks, which cause the spoilers on one wing to

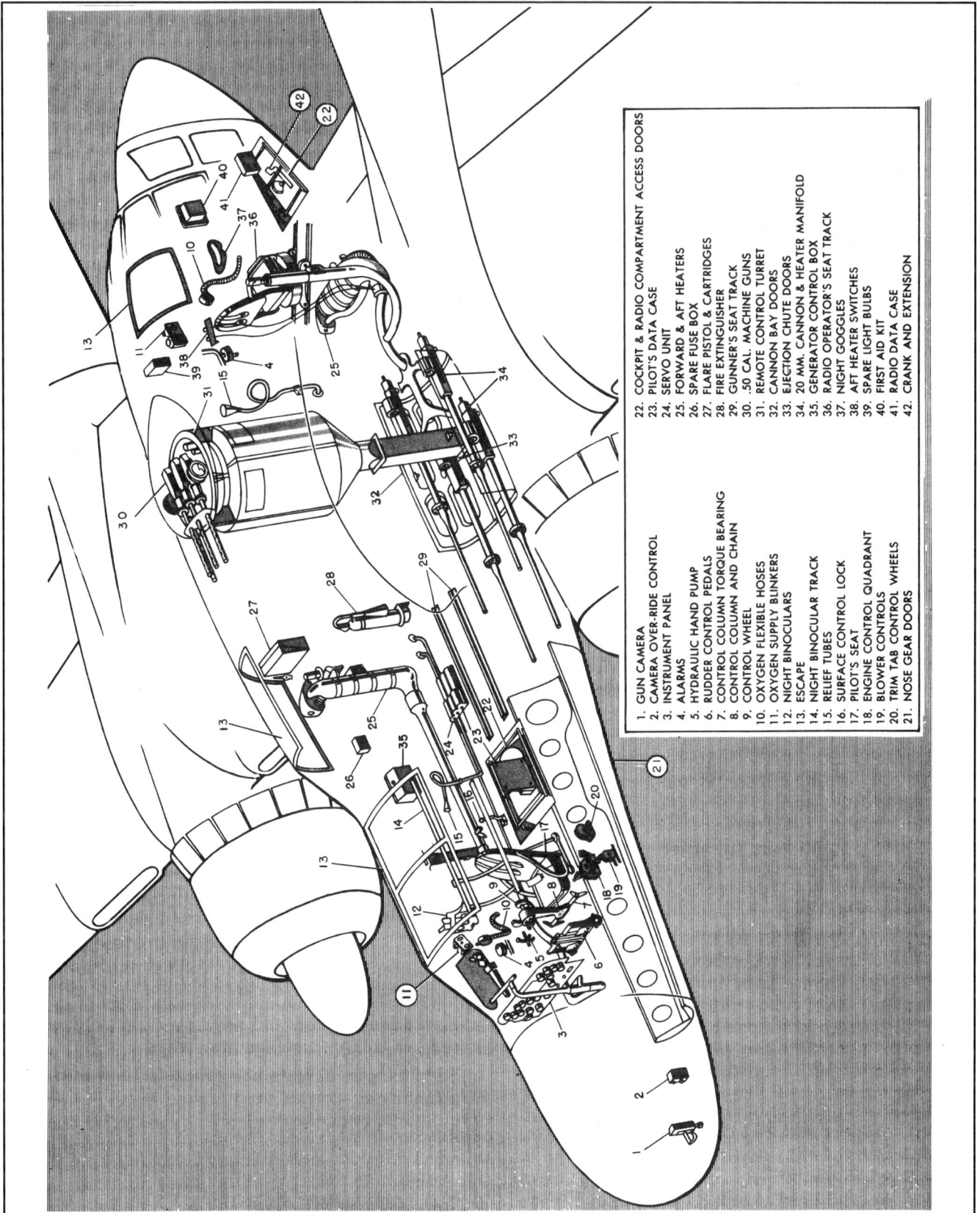

1. GUN CAMERA
2. CAMERA OVER-RIDE CONTROL
3. INSTRUMENT PANEL
4. ALARMS
5. HYDRAULIC HAND PUMP
6. RUDDER CONTROL PEDALS
7. CONTROL COLUMN TORQUE BEARING
8. CONTROL COLUMN AND CHAIN
9. CONTROL WHEEL
10. OXYGEN FLEXIBLE HOSES
11. OXYGEN SUPPLY BLINKERS
12. NIGHT BINOCULARS
13. ESCAPE
14. NIGHT BINOCULAR TRACK
15. RELIEF TUBES
16. SURFACE CONTROL LOCK
17. PILOT'S SEAT
18. ENGINE CONTROL QUADRANT
19. BLOWER CONTROLS
20. TRIM TAB CONTROL WHEELS
21. NOSE GEAR DOORS
22. COCKPIT & RADIO COMPARTMENT ACCESS DOORS
23. PILOT'S DATA CASE
24. SERVO UNIT
25. FORWARD & AFT HEATERS
26. SPARE FUSE BOX
27. FLARE PISTOL & CARTRIDGES
28. FIRE EXTINGUISHER
29. GUNNER'S SEAT TRACK
30. .50 CAL. MACHINE GUNS
31. REMOTE CONTROL TURRET
32. CANNON BAY DOORS
33. EJECTION CHUTE DOORS
34. 20 MM. CANNON & HEATER MANIFOLD
35. GENERATOR CONTROL BOX
36. RADIO OPERATOR'S SEAT TRACK
37. NIGHT GOGGLES
38. AFT HEATER SWITCHES
39. SPARE LIGHT BULBS
40. FIRST AID KIT
41. RADIO DATA CASE
42. CRANK AND EXTENSION

On routine inspections by the crew chief, the total number of checks in the crew compartments numbered 42. These were not done after each flight, but if anything was written up by a crew member, it was handled immediately or before the next flight. There were printed procedures for the 200-hour and the 400-hour inspections in these areas.

There were good days and bad days on the assembly line. These P-61Bs suffered substantial damage to their nose sections and tail cones as a result of a conveyor accident. (Northrop)

rise 65 degrees, while those on the other wing lower 28 degrees. Adjustable push-pull rods connect the differential bellcranks to the spoilers, and aileron quadrants connect directly to the ailerons by means of adjustable push-pull rods.

Conventional, adjustable foot pedals control the rudders. Two cables extend aft from each of the two pedals, providing an independent system for each rudder. A buss cable connects the two pedals, running on both sides of the cockpit and through both tailbooms to bellcranks in the empennage, from which they extend aft to the rudder horns. The right rudder cable system connects through the automatic pilot servo unit.

The automatic servo unit consists of three cylinders cast *en bloc* with piston rods extending at each end, that connects directly to the main control cables of the aircraft. A manually operated by-pass valve engages or disengages the automatic pilot. Spring-loaded relief valves are built into each hydraulic surface control, to permit the pilot to overpower the automatic pilot by applying increased force to the controls.

Most of the aircraft that were designed and built during the war, had a certain air of sophistication about them and all were complicated pieces of machinery. Probably the most technically advanced aircraft to come out of the war was the B-29 Superfortress, which was the only aircraft designed and built during the war that had a significant impact during the early Cold War years, when jets dominated. The priority for gun turrets favored the B-29, hence the P-61 was produced in large numbers, without its .50-caliber gun turret.

The technical data above does not cover all facets of the Black Widow's anatomy. It was a fantastic airframe and one of the outstanding engineering accomplishments to emerge from the United States in World War II.

WARBIRDTECH
S E R I E S

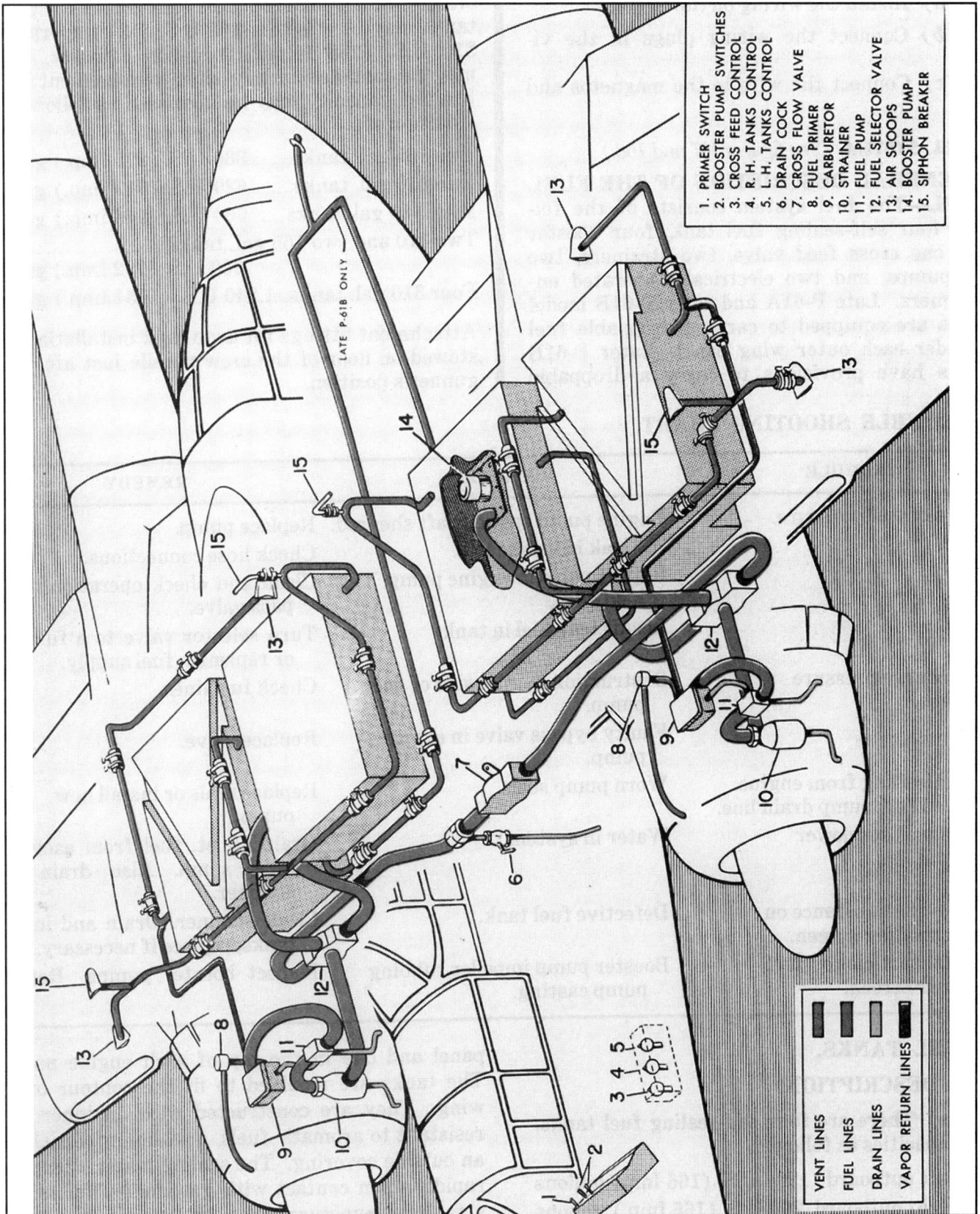

1. PRIMER SWITCH
2. BOOSTER PUMP SWITCHES
3. CROSS FEED CONTROL
4. R. H. TANKS CONTROL
5. L. H. TANKS CONTROL
6. DRAIN COCK
7. CROSS FLOW VALVE
8. FUEL PRIMER
9. CARBURETOR
10. STRAINER
11. FUEL PUMP
12. FUEL SELECTOR VALVE
13. AIR SCOOPS
14. BOOSTER PUMP
15. SIPHON BREAKER

VENT LINES
FUEL LINES
DRAIN LINES
VAPOR RETURN LINES

LATE P-61B ONLY

The P-61 had a very elaborate fuel system, with all internal tanks interconnected. The pilot could shift fuel from any fuel tank to another at any altitude. In this case, the droppable tanks are not included. The lines were constantly kept under 6 to 8 PSI to prevent vapor lock.

Flying the P-61

HIGHLY SKILLED CREW MAKE THE WIDOW STING

The training programs initiated by the Army Air Corps during World War II were of monumental proportions. Between December 1942 and August 1945, more than 35,000 day fighter pilots were trained. In contrast, only 485 night fighter crews were trained during this same period. The training syllabus for the latter was much more complex.

Precise attention was given to crew teamwork. The normal crew for the P-70 and the P-61 consisted of a pilot, radar operator and gunner. The night fighters operated alone and their best chance of success was to have well-trained crews that could function as a unit. In most cases, each Black Widow crew worked a designated sector, alone. With the help of GCI (Ground Control Intercept), they stalked their targets, made the visual identification and took them out. It was the way they were trained to fight.

The problem of crew teamwork did not exist in day fighter training, thus their emphasis was more on maximum individual proficiency and precise coordination among the pilots of each squadron and group.

Looking out of the front windscreen of the XP-61. This was taken in July 1943, two months before the first P-61s were delivered to the training facility at Orlando, Florida. (Roy Wolford)

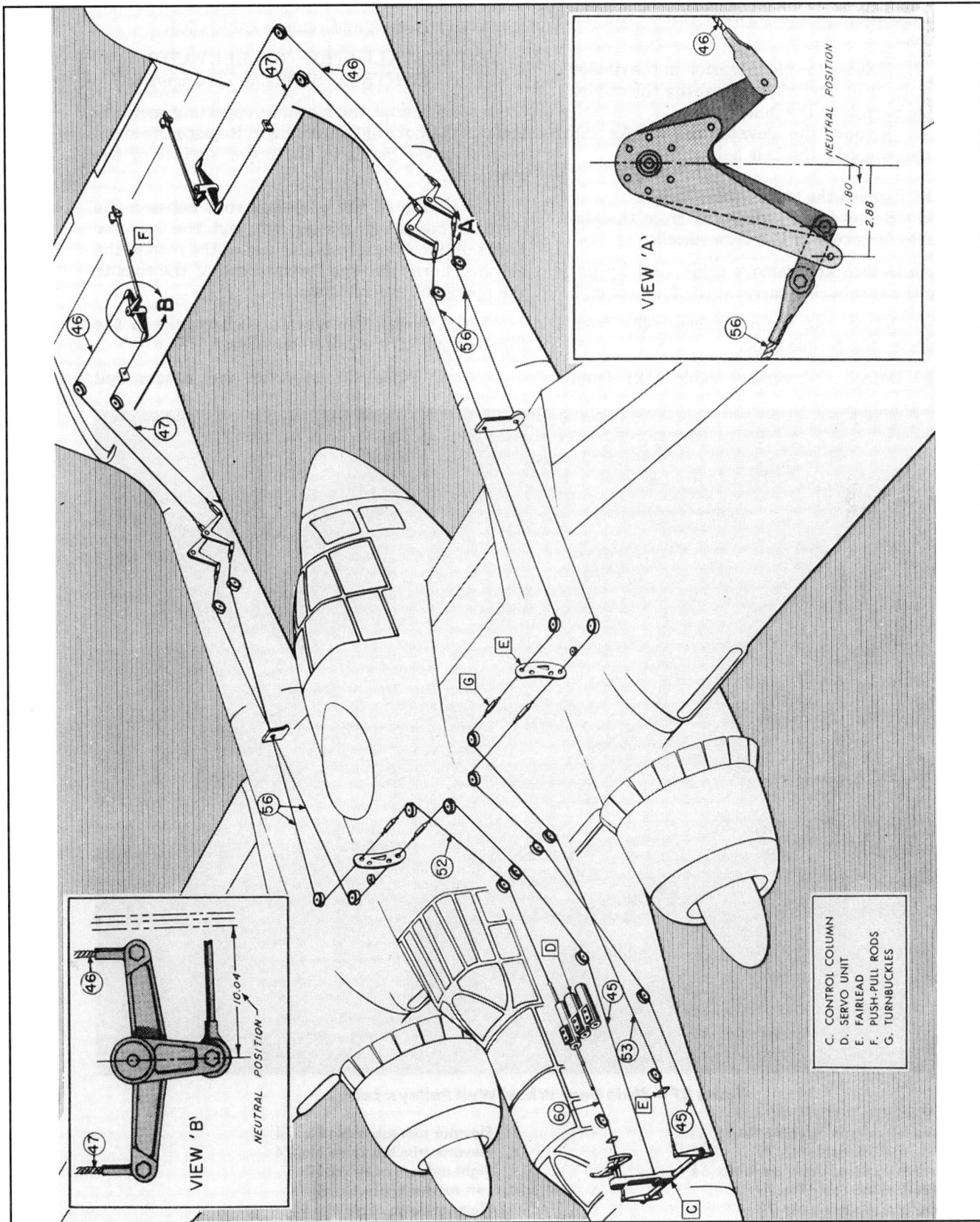

VIEW 'A'

NEUTRAL POSITION

1.80
2.88

VIEW 'B'

10.04

NEUTRAL POSITION

C. CONTROL COLUMN
D. SERVO UNIT
E. FAIRLEAD
F. PUSH-PULL RODS
G. TURNBUCKLES

The elevator control system included two complete and independent systems of cables, push-rods and bell cranks. Both systems were controlled from the cranks attached to the ends of the control column torque tube. Each system ran aft separately through the engine nacelles.

The left lower quadrant of the P-61 cockpit. The pilots were required to know every inch of this cockpit in the dark. With the special low lighting of the instruments and the pilot's keen night vision, it was easy to read all of the instruments. (Gerald Balzer)

Night fighter training differed from day training in several ways. Night fighter pilots flew in an entirely different environment, so instrument flying, night formation exercises and night gunnery were stressed.

At the old Fighter Command School at Orlando, Florida, the very first night fighter crews were trained. The nucleus of the program was formed by the instructors, who had been trained by the RAF over in England. By this time, the British had become masters in the art of night warfare in the air.

The only aircraft available for training when the program started were the converted Douglas A-20 Havocs, which were designated as P-70s. The Radar Operators received their early training in the Beech AT-11s. In September 1943, the first P-61 arrived at the training facility in Orlando. This signaled the first time that all three of the night fighter crew members (pilot, R/O and gunner) could begin working as a cohesive unit.

Four months after the first Black Widow arrived, the training pro-

gram was moved to Hammer Field in San Diego, California, which would be the only base to teach night fighter tactics. The three-man crews that they turned out stayed together for their entire tour of duty in the forward areas, only separating due to an accident or enemy action.

The pilots that arrived at Hammer Field for training already had their wings and carried the rank of 2nd Lieutenant or Flight Officer. They also had completed some extensive training at Douglas, Arizona, in

ELEVATOR *UP*
LIMIT STOP

29° *UP* FOR AIRPLANES
42-5510 AND SUBS.

28° *UP* FOR AIRPLANES
42-5485 TO 42-5509

12°

17° 30'

NEUTRAL   VERTICAL

FW'D LIMIT

AFT LIMIT

-12°   -14½°-

CONTROL COLUMN
(NEUTRAL POSITION)

NOTE

THE CONTROL COLUMN CAN BE
PULLED BACK TO ITS LIMIT OF
28° AFT OF NEUTRAL ONLY BY
DEFLECTING THE SPRING TAB.
IF THE SPRING TAB IS *NOT* DE-
FLECTED, THE ELEVATOR *UP* STOP
WILL HIT WHILE A GAP STILL
REMAINS AT THE CONTROL
COLUMN STOP. THERE IS NO
STOP AT THE ELEVATOR FOR THE
ELEVATOR *DOWN* POSITION.

CONTROL COLUMN

CONTROL
COLUMN FORWARD

GAP WITH ELEV. FULL *UP*
AND SPRING TAB *NOT* DEFLECTED.

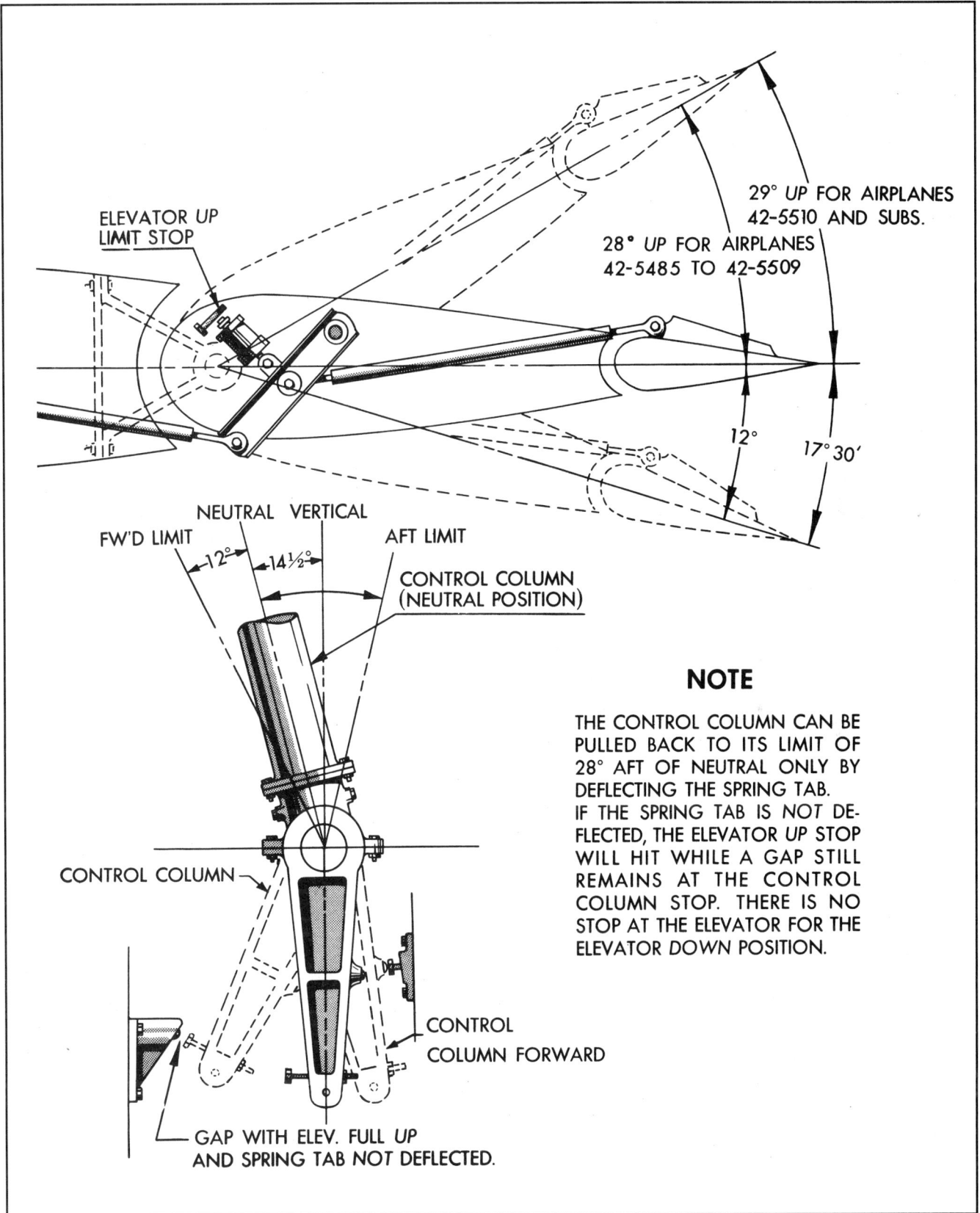

Diagram shows the spring tab mechanism that allows full 28-degree deflection of the elevator system. The early models of the P-61A did not have the spring tabs installed. The control column can be flexed only to its 28 degree maximum.

4803-102 NORTHROP
COCKPIT-LEFT SIDE-XP61

The lower left area of the pilot's panel clearly shows the controls for the throttle, fuel mixture and fuel valve controls. The tanks were all connected, so the pilot could shift fuel to any tank necessary. (Roy Wolford)

the B-25 bomber, mostly advanced courses in instrument flying. These credentials only allowed the pilot to advance up one notch in the training syllabus. Once at Hammer Field, the pilot would have to go through more instrument flying in ground school and 20 hours in the air. His training would all but begin again!

In a large majority of the cases, the pilot and radar operator became lifelong friends. Where compatibility was lacking, the pairs were broken up and realigned with more suitable individuals. High-ranking

officers who were involved in the training process all agreed that the closer the pilot and radar operator, the better chances they had to destroy the enemy and get back to base safely.

While still in the basic training phase, the pilot/radar operator team were given several hours in the TB-26, which was a modified Martin Marauder. It was big enough to allow an instructor pilot and instructor radar observer on-board. The one-on-one instruction proved to be very effective. This training segment also marked the first time

that the team was allowed to fly tactical interception missions in the P-61.

After three months of night fighter basic training, the crews moved to nearby Hayward Field for an intense one-month period of high and low altitude night flying, advanced interception tactics, evasive maneuvers and, of the utmost importance, close coordination with Ground Control Intercept (GCI). Once trained, an average mission would go something like this:

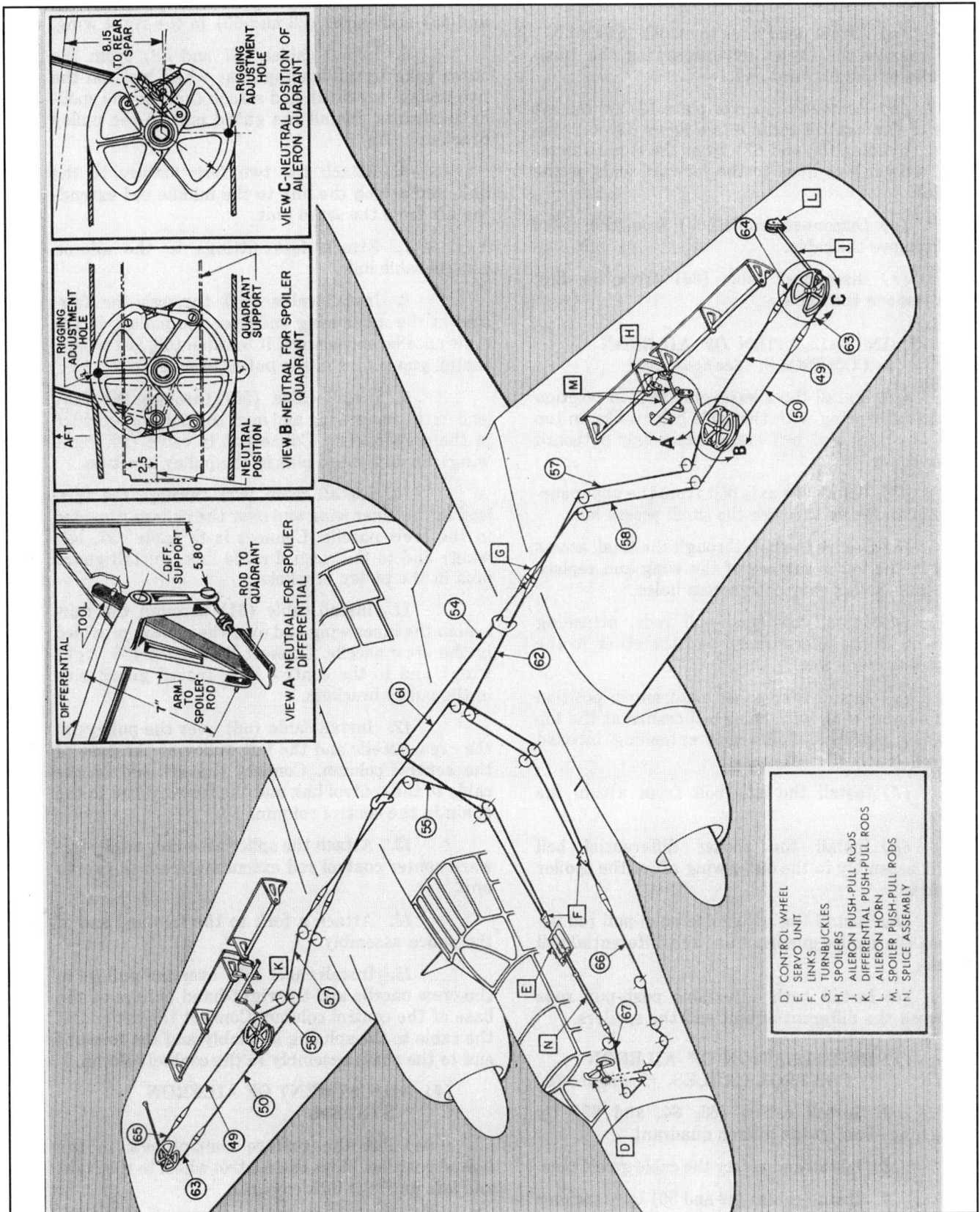

VIEW **C** - NEUTRAL POSITION OF AILERON QUADRANT

RIGGING ADJUSTMENT HOLE

8.15 TO REAR SPAR

VIEW **B** - NEUTRAL FOR SPOILER QUADRANT

RIGGING ADJUSTMENT HOLE

QUADRANT SUPPORT

AFT

NEUTRAL POSITION

2.5

VIEW **A** - NEUTRAL FOR SPOILER DIFFERENTIAL

DIFFERENTIAL

TOOL

DIFF. SUPPORT

5.80

ROD TO QUADRANT

7" ARM TO SPOILER ROD

D. CONTROL WHEEL
E. SERVO UNIT
F. LINKS
G. TURNBUCKLES
H. SPOILERS
J. AILERON PUSH-PULL RODS
K. DIFFERENTIAL PUSH-PULL RODS
L. AILERON HORN
M. SPOILER PUSH-PULL RODS
N. SPLICE ASSEMBLY

On both the P-61 A and B, a combination of the spoiler and conventional type of aileron was used. Movement was controlled through the chain and sprocket in the control column. The cables run aft along the wing and right side walls of the cockpit, then outboard through the wings to the spoiler quadrants and then on to the aileron quadrants.

P-61 BLACK WIDOW

47

The right panel shows the recognition light keying switch, radio control box and radio transmitter. All of these controls were located on the opposite side of the throttles. (Northrop)

Strapping In For the Mission:

Before a P-61 pilot and his crew could even begin to think about climbing into the cockpit for a mission, they place dark-red-lensed night-adjustment goggles on about 30 to 40 minutes prior to going out to the aircraft. Usually, this time period is used to discuss what they have learned at the briefing and to review any adverse weather conditions or unusual enemy activity that they might encounter. At the end of this short adjustment period, their eyes have been sensitized to the dark and from this time on, they will go out of their way to avoid anything that would diminish their night vision.

After the ride or walk out to the aircraft, the crew climbs into their respective compartments. Each individual knows his particular cockpit area so well that a total loss of light would not hinder his ability to function, especially the pilot.

From the pilot's standpoint, the cockpit check is as vital as knowing how to fly the plane. The pilot's first procedure is to inspect his Plexiglas canopy for dirt or anything that could cause distortion. To miss something that might reflect any stray light could cut down on visibility by at least 50 percent.

After the canopy check, the pilot ensures that the crew chief has closed and secured the doors to each compartment. Then, with the exception of the heater and cannon relay switches, the circuit breakers and switches on the generator control panel are turned on. Scanning the instrument panel, he makes sure that none of the cover glasses are broken or loose.

WARBIRD**TECH**
S E R I E S

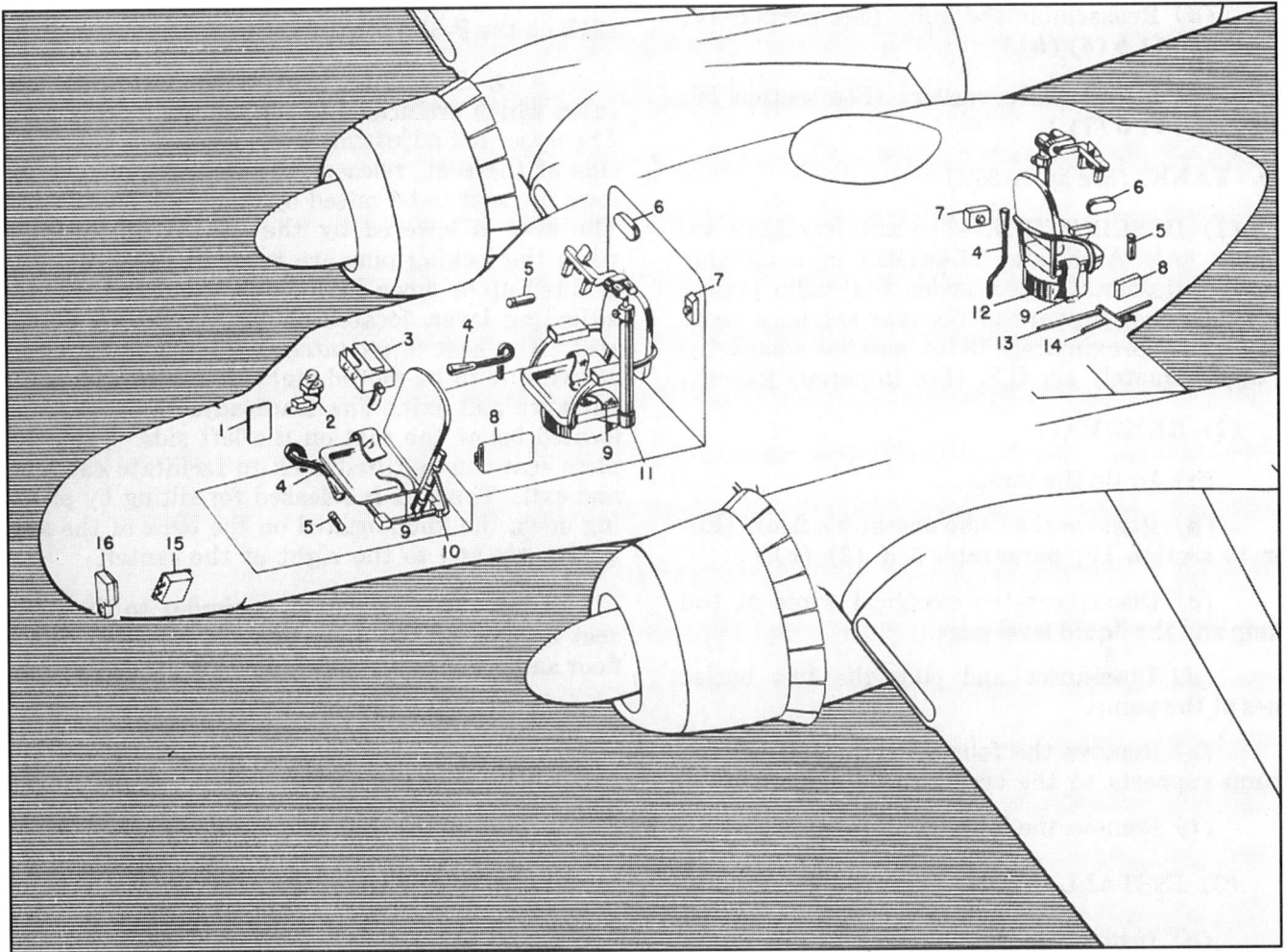

(Above) This cutaway shows all 24 pieces of equipment that were necessary for the successful operation of the P-61. This total was a combination from all three crew compartments. The most important items included the special seats, night binoculars, standard gunsight for the pilot and sighting devices for both the gunner and radar operator.

The gunner's compartment with its canopy removed exposes armor plate and the aiming device for the .50-caliber machine gun turret. The outside arc of the propellers was just inches away from a point on the crew nacelle that was halfway between the pilot and gunner's compartment. (Roy Wolford)

The entrance ladder that accessed the forward pilot/gunner's compartment was located at the rear of the nose wheel cutout. Note the nose wheel mud guard, prevented large amounts of moisture and debris from slinging into the wheel well. With the amount of critical wiring that transited through this area, the guard prevented a tremendous amount of maintenance. (Roy Wolford)

The clock, altimeter, pressure gauges and the fuel and oxygen tanks are checked to make sure they are registering properly. The pilot releases the surface control lock, which makes it possible to open the throttles, then sets the parking brakes.

Now the pilot is ready for the pre-start check; he inspects the cockpit all the way around, starting at the extreme left of the console. Sets all the trim tabs at neutral and sets the fuel selector valves to the outboard tanks with the crossfeed valve off. Make sure the feather switches

An early production P-61A-1-NO flies over California. Only 45 of this series were built, and this type was heavily flown in the training of advanced night fighter crews over this same terrain at night. (Northrop)

WARBIRD**TECH**
SERIES

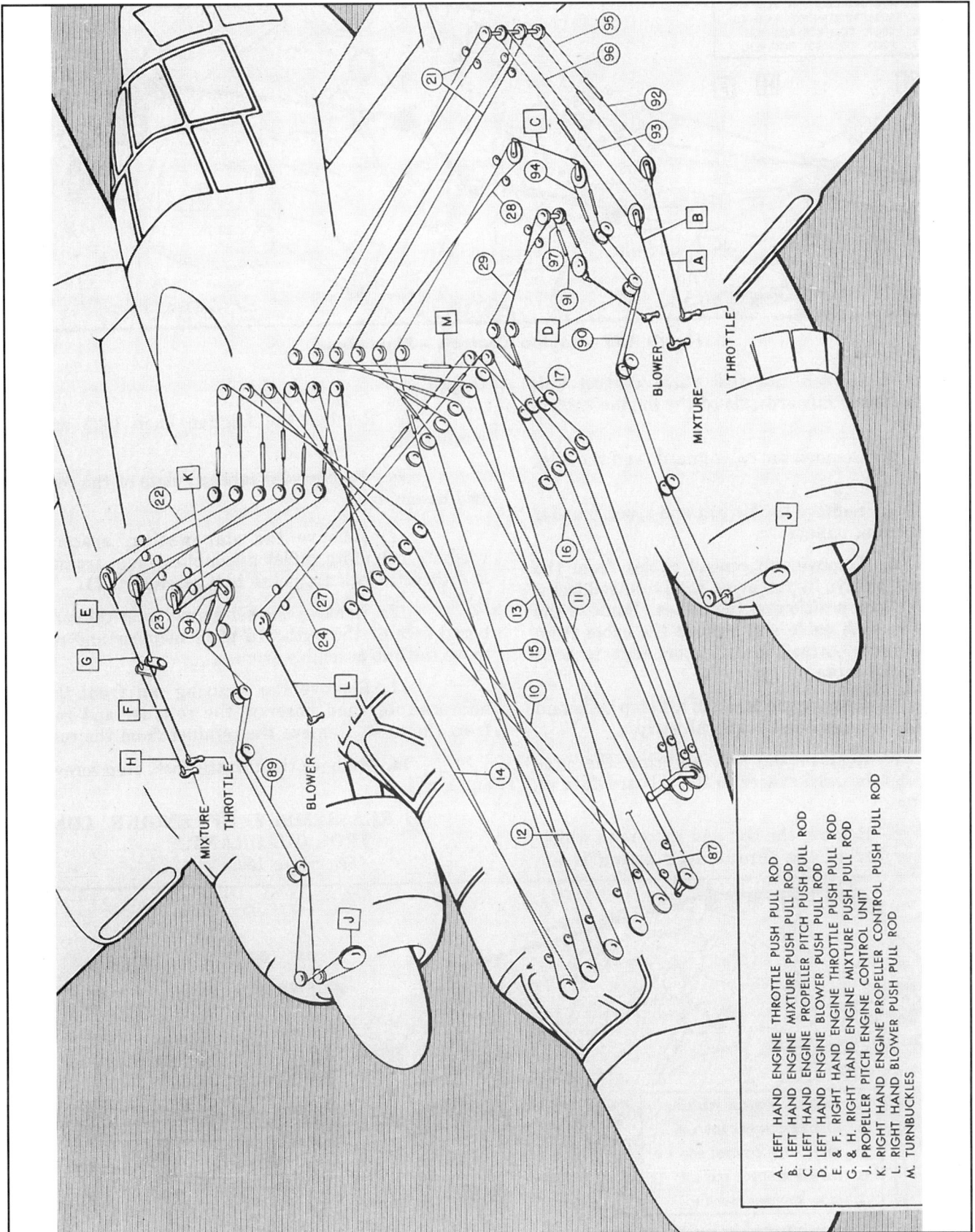

The legend in the lower right box reads:

A. LEFT HAND ENGINE THROTTLE PUSH PULL ROD
B. LEFT HAND ENGINE MIXTURE PUSH PULL ROD
C. LEFT HAND ENGINE PROPELLER PITCH PUSH PULL ROD
D. LEFT HAND ENGINE BLOWER PUSH PULL ROD
E. & F. RIGHT HAND ENGINE THROTTLE PUSH PULL ROD
G. & H. RIGHT HAND ENGINE MIXTURE PUSH PULL ROD
J. PROPELLER PITCH ENGINE CONTROL UNIT
K. RIGHT HAND ENGINE PROPELLER CONTROL PUSH PULL ROD
L. RIGHT HAND ENGINE BLOWER PUSH PULL ROD
M. TURNBUCKLES

The engine and propeller controls were, perhaps, the most complicated system within the aircraft. If there was a malfunction, it was very time-consuming to fix the problem.

6726-063 NORTHROP
50 CAL. TURRET-MUZZLE
BLAST MARKS FWD. ENCLOSURE

Night vision was critical to the entire P-61 crew. Two factors could severely damage this vision, for a brief, if not fatal, period: lightning and the muzzle blast from the .50-caliber guns. In this picture, you can see the close proximity to the gunner's compartment. (Gerald Balzer)

are in the normal position and the propeller selector switches are on constant speed, where they should always be kept except in an emergency.

The pilot places the throttles

Looking to the rear behind the gunner's station you can see the gunner's sighting equipment, which has swung over to the left side of the compartment. Also note the partition between the gunner and the radar operator's station. The .50 caliber machine gun turret was housed in this space. (Roy Wolford)

one-third open and the mixture controls at idle cut-off. Propeller control levers are all the way forward. If the flaps are not up already, they are put up as soon as the engines are running. Check to make sure the landing gear handle is latched down firmly. Open all the cowl flaps, returning the levers to locked. Be certain that the oil pressure for the automatic pilot is off and that the automatic pilot itself is disengaged. Check both VHF radio switches to see that they are off and be sure the identification light switches are in the off position.

The pilot is now ready to start the engines. Before turning on the switches, though, the crew chief pulls the prop through at least four revolutions. This removes the oil that has drained into the lower cylinders of each engine since the aircraft was last flown. The ignition switch for the starboard engine is turned on only after the pilot has yelled

(Above) The access ladder and hatch to the radar operator's station, which was completely separated from the pilot and gunner' compartment by all of the radio equipment and the .50-caliber top turret. This picture was of a YP-61 was taken at the factory by Northrop photographer Roy Wolford.

Aerial shot of #25501 over the mountains of California in 1944. This aircraft was a P-61A-1-NO, which was in the first series produced after the production of the YP-61. (Roy Wolford)

"clear" and the ground crew member has answered that the props are clear. The right starter is energized for the proper length of time. For the final five seconds of this procedure, the engine is primed.

Now, he right starter is engaged and the prop begins to turn over. As soon as it fires, the mixture control is turned over to auto-rich. The starter remains engaged until the engine is turning over smoothly. The engine is run at 600 to 800 RPM until the oil pressure registers. At this time, the RPM are increased to between 1,000 to 1,200. The same

(Above) The photographer readies his camera to take shots of maintenance work on a P-61 in a hanger. More than likely, these photos were destined to upgrade illustrations for the maintenance manual. Note the B-26 Marauder parked outside; this was probably one of the TB-26s that was used in advanced night fighter training. (Northrop)

Myriad toggle switches on the far left of the front panel in the pilot's compartment would be operated by the left hand, which usually was at the throttle. The pilot's right hand stayed on the control column. (Gerald Balzer)

procedure is repeated for the port engine.

In the "P-61A Flight Manual," five major rules must be adhered to by the pilot:

1. Wing flaps should not be fully extended at speeds of more than 175 MPH indicated airspeed (IAS)

2. Landing gear should not be extended at speeds of more than 175 MPH (IAS).

3. Landing lights should not be extended at speeds of more than 140 MPH (IAS).

4. Maximum diving speed to be red-lined at a speed of 415 MPH.

5. Never permit the auto-pilot to control the aircraft at speeds of less than 150 MPH (IAS).

A combat-experienced P-61 crew with its flight gear, a 6th Night Fighter Squadron trio, was photographed on Saipan prior to flying a combat mission. Left to right are Lieutenant Jean Desclos (radar operator), 1st Lieutenant James Crumley (pilot) and Private Otis O'Hara (gunner). These crews stayed together for their entire training and combat tours. (Jerome Hansen)

A P-61 gets run up at night before an advanced training mission over California. The aircrews were exposed to heavy doses of low-level flying and night attack procedures when they made intercepts of other aircraft. When they graduated from advanced training, they were second to none in the art of night flying. (Northrop)

One could picture this scene over enemy skies in total darkness. Note the pilot's and gunner's field of vision along with the top .50 turret and four 20mm cannon in the belly of this YP-61. This would have been too close for a safe kill if the Black Widow had been in a hostile environment. The firepower of the P-61 was awesome. (National Archives)

It was very important that the props be manually turned over by the crew chief, or whomever, for at least four revolutions prior to starting the engine. This motion moved the oil into the upper cylinders after idleness had allowed it to drain into the lower cylinders. Only after this procedure has been completed can the pilot safely turn on the ignition switch. (U.S. Air Force)

Figure 195F — Pilot's Cockpit — Left Side (P-61B)

1. SPARE GUN SIGHT LAMPS
2. PANEL LIGHT
3. LANDING GEAR WARNING HORN RELEASE
4. NIGHT BINOCULAR TRACK
5. PROPELLER CONTROL PANEL
6. ENGINE CONTROL QUADRANT
7. WING FLAP CONTROL QUADRANT
8. WATER INJECTION POWER SWITCH
9. EMERGENCY AIR BRAKE PRESSURE GAGE
10. FLAP UPLOCK WARNING LIGHT

11. IGNITION CONTROL BOX
12. CROSS FEED VALVE CONTROL
13. RIGHT FUEL TANK CONTROL
14. ENGINE CONTROL QUADRANT FRICTION ADJUSTMENT
15. LEFT FUEL TANK CONTROL
16. SUPERCHARGER CONTROL
17. RUDDER TRIM TAB CONTROL
18. LANDING GEAR EMERGENCY RELEASE
19. LANDING GEAR EMERGENCY RELEASE SUPPORT
20. ELEVATOR TRIM TAB CONTROL

Basically, the left side of the pilot's compartment was devoted to controlling the engines. Before the night fighter pilot would receive his first flight in the P-61, he would know every item in the cockpit blindfolded. In a combat situation, he could make all the necessary adjustments in a close pursuit without ever taking his eyes off the gunsight.

Figure 195G — Pilot's Cockpit — Right Side (P-61B)

1. OXYGEN PRESSURE GAGE
2. RECOGNITION LIGHT CONTROL BOX
3. BOMB AND TANK RELEASE CONTROL
4. AN-APN-1 RADIO CONTROL
5. COMMAND RADIO CONTROL BOX
6. AN-APS-13 RADIO CONTROLS
7. LIAISON RADIO CONTROL BOX
8. PANEL LIGHT
9. RADIO JACK BOX
10. FLEXIBLE OXYGEN TUBE
11. DE-ICER VALVE CONTROL
12. OXYGEN REGULATOR
13. CHEMICAL TANK CONTROLS
14. BC-1206 RANGE RECEIVER
15. PILOT'S ENCLOSURE DEFROSTER TUBE
16. DEFROSTER TUBE HOLDER
17. BOMB CONTROLS
18. IDENTIFICATION RADIO CONTROL BOX
19. DESTRUCTOR
20. AUTOMATIC PILOT MASTER CONTROL
21. PILOT'S VENTILATOR
22. HYDRAULIC HAND PUMP
23. HYDRAULIC HAND PUMP SELECTOR VALVE
24. AUTOMATIC PILOT PRESSURE CONTROL

(Opposite page) Closure on an enemy aircraft depended on the speed of the target. Once a visual identification was made, the pilot had his face in the gunsight and his right thumb on the firing button located to the right of the bomb and tank release. His left hand was always on the throttles. If the closure rate was too great, the Black Widow could overshoot and become the victim in a matter of seconds.

Figure 195H — Pilot's Cockpit Front (P-61B)

1. CORRECTION CARD HOLDER
2. CLEAR VIEW PANEL
3. PANEL LIGHT
4. PILOT'S GUN SIGHT
5. RUDDER PEDAL
6. IGNITION CONTROL PANEL

7. ELECTRICAL CONTROL PANEL
8. BOMB-TANK RELEASE
9. RUDDER PEDAL
10. LANDING GEAR SELECTOR VALVE CONTROL
11. PROPELLER CONTROL
12. MIXTURE CONTROL

ARMAMENT 5 AND RADAR

Three things made the P-61 the deadliest aircraft in the nocturnal arena. First and foremost was the quality of its aircrews. If you were to rate them on sheer skills, they probably would be about two notches above excellent. Simply put, they were the result of the best training program in the world. The remaining two advantages were good radar and brute firepower. This trio of traits combined to shoot down some of the best aircraft and pilots that the Japanese and Germans had.

Any aircraft that gained a reputation for itself, during the war, had to have more than speed and sleek lines. They had to have a heavy knock-out punch, either

This is as close as you'll get to seeing just what devastation the P-61 could dole out. All eight guns were firing tracer ammo in this demo and seeing is believing. Note that the nose gear is up, which allows the cannon to fire.
(Roy Wolford)

14651-055 NORTHROP CAL. 50 & 20 MM TRACER TEST-NIGHT FIRING P-61 B

Firing tracers on the bore sight range at night. This angle shows the pattern of .50-caliber and 20MM rounds reaching out for an enemy aircraft. The 20MM casings are falling into the V-shaped collector below the aircraft.
(Roy Wolford)

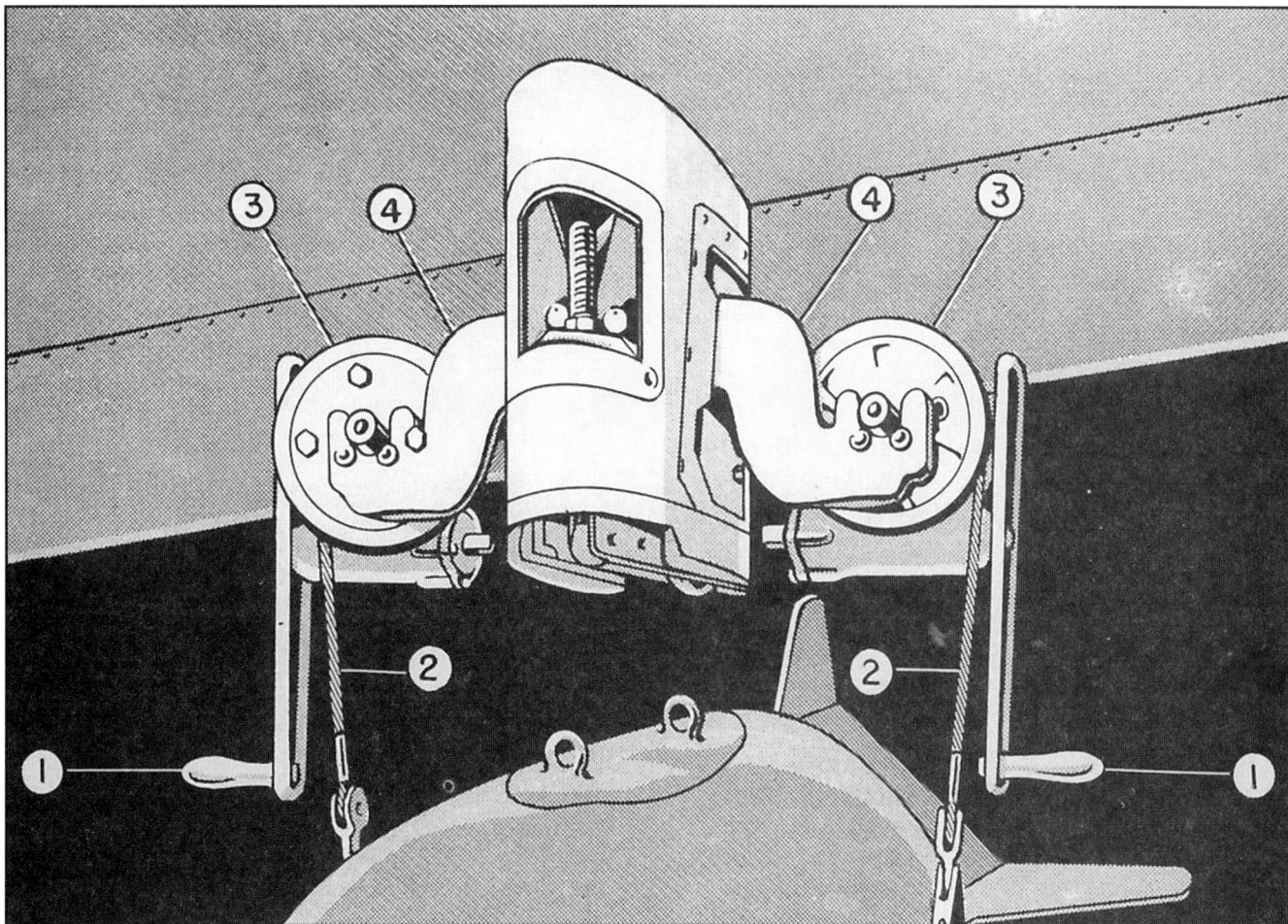

(Above) The pylons that were installed in the final P-61As and early P-61Bs were capable of carrying bombs, napalm, fuel and chemical tanks. If fuel tanks or bombs were being removed while the aircraft was on the ground, the selector switch inside the cockpit was turned to salvo and the bomb release switch on the pilot's control wheel was pressed. Once separated, the device was slowly lowered to ground level.

This more panoramic view shows the turret being lowered into its place in a XP-61 that is on the final leg of the assembly line. The Pratt & Whitney engines have already been put in place and the outer segment of the wings are just being attached.
(Gerald Balzer)

NORTHROP
P-61 BLACK WIDOW

The 1,600-pound General Electric turret is lowered into its proper position in an XP-61 at the Northrop factory. This photo was taken to demonstrate the correct way to remove or place the turret in a P-61 and would later be incorporated into one of the procedural manuals.
(Gerald Balzer)

4499-092 NORTHROP
METHOD OF HOISTING

against enemy aircraft or targets on the ground. The P-61 was blessed with more than its share of destructive capabilities, with four 20MM cannon and four .50-caliber machine guns. With all eight of these guns firing from the centerline, they could destroy anything they hit.

The initial plans had called for the Black Widow to have both the cannon and machine guns, but two factors cut this configuration short of its mark and many P-61s left the factory without machine guns. The top turret machine guns caused some violent buffeting when the guns were elevated or rotated in azimuth.

12303-114 NORTHROP
4 GUN TURRET INSTAL. WITH GUN
VANES & MK-1 FLASH ELIMINATORS.

One of the suggestions that was made by the original test and evaluation team was to provide flash suppression for the .50-caliber guns. As this picture shows, the Mark-1 flash eliminators have been installed.
(Roy Wolford)

WARBIRD**TECH**
SERIES

Turret buffeting proved to be a significant problem with the P-61. Numerous configurations were tested and none really solved the problem. The coolie hat design, shown here, seemed to work best, but it disintegrated under the pressure of a high speed-dive. (Northrop)

Another view of the coolie hat design at the Northrop Plant in California. (Northrop)

Another design attempt to solve the buffeting problem was the beavertail. (Northrop)

One of the designs that was used to test the turret buffeting problem was this one with a circular laminated wooden dish. It was not successful. (Northrop)

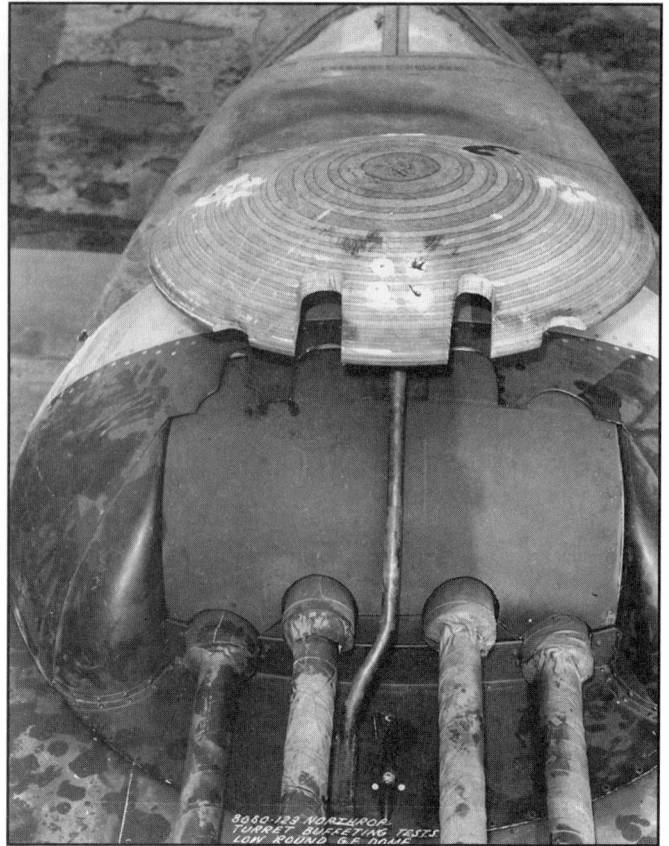

Many tests and configurations were experimented with, but none seemed to solve the buffeting problem. A "coolie hat" configuration seemed to work better than others, but when the speed of the aircraft increased to levels it would have reached in aerial combat, the apparatus broke off. When the turret was turned sideways with the guns aiming off at an angle, the airflow was severely distorted and the buffeting increased.

The second factor was that General Electric, the turret manufacturer, had problems keeping up with the orders for B-29 turrets, which had a higher priority. The Northrop project for the P-61 had a government priority rating of A-1-B, which was almost a top priority, but not quite good enough. The level would have (text continued on page 71)

Basically, this is the same beavertail configuration as several that were tested. This one had been painted and installed over a differently shaped turret. (Northrop)

WARBIRDTECH
S E R I E S

FRAMED IN FULL COLOR

It would have been impossible to shoot the P-61 while it was working. The night shift does not lend itself well to living color. Color photography was extremely rare in World War II and of all the aircraft in frontline inventory, the Black Widow was probably the least photographed.

However, thanks to the people at Northrop and the few that had 35MM cameras immediately after the war, there are some very good color transparencies in existence.

All of these have framed the P-61 while it was off-duty. Though most shots show the aircraft as being rather run-down and war-weary, its distinct and sleek lines would be hard to cover up.

The small number of color pictures that are available, must be preserved to insure that future generations become aware of just how magnificent this night fighter was and how much it contributed to the war effort in all theatres.

Worn out and still flying, these P-61s were photographed over Okinawa in the late 1940s. All of these aircraft had seen combat during the war and were just waiting to be replaced by the F-82. Flying in bad weather and the natural elements had taken its toll on the paint job on two of these 4th All Weather squadron aircraft. (Doug Smith)

After the war ended, the 6th Night Fighter Squadron was pulled back to Wheeler Field in Hawaii. This P-61B already had the large numeral painted on the nose which signified aircraft of the 6th. (Jack Hahn)

P-61 crew members hoist their luggage after a brief stopover at Fort Carson in Canada. This base was used for refueling most of the military aircraft that were enroute from the Northwest United States to Alaska. This aircraft was assigned to the 449th All Weather Squadron. Note the size of the Black Widow, which was the largest fighter built in the United States during World War II. (Tadas Spelis)

The 421st Night Fighter Squadron moved from Ie Shima to Itazuke AB, Japan on 25 November 1945. Their aircraft had the spinners painted yellow. This picture was taken over Japan in late 1946. The 421st became the 68th All Weather squadron in 1948. (Gerald Bliss)

A P-61A-10 rests on the ramp at the Northrop plant in California. This was one of the last "A" models produced and the "B"'s were soon to be coming off the production lines. The Dash-10 series did not have the .50 calibre turrets. (Roy Wolford)

WARBIRDTECH
SERIES

A Northrop P-61B-2-NO that was used to test the new 310 gallon drop tanks. The tests were conducted by Northrop personnel. The chase plane that the photo was taken from was also a P-61. (Roy Wolford)

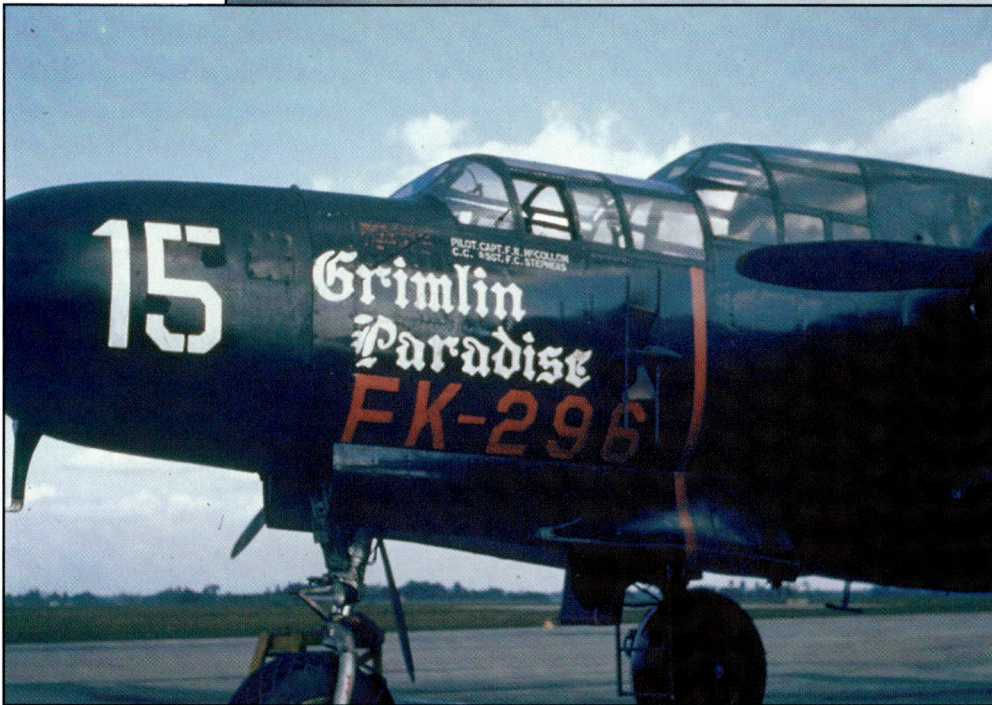

Grimlin Paradise, a P-61 assigned to the 339th All Weather squadron at Johnson AB, Japan during the early postwar years. These aircraft would soon be replaced by the North American F-82, which would see combat at the beginning of the Korean War. (Martin Bambrick)

Northrop was a front runner in designing a long range escort fighter that could stay with the B-29's on their long missions to Japan. However the project did not get very far. Only two models were built and one was destroyed in an accident. This XP-61E was shown in flight over California in early 1945. (Roy Wolford)

The pipeline of replacement aircraft, to the Pacific Theatre, had to go through Hawaii. This new P-61B, with top turret, had been delivered via ship to the first major staging point. It has been assembled and awaits the ferry crew that will fly it to the forward bases. At this time, Iwo Jima had been captured, so the front lines were moving closer to Japan. (Leo Goff)

This Black Widow was the third production model in the P-61A-1-NO series. It was being tested by a Northrop test pilot before being accepted by the Army Air Corps. Note the dull olive drab paint scheme which signified some of the early "A" models. The 6th NFS received some of these OD aircraft. (Roy Wolford)

This Black Widow was a P-61B-20 in which Northrop built eighty-four of. The Dash-20 series provided some of the final replacement aircraft sent to front line squadrons before the war ended. This ship was serving with the 339th All Weather squadron at Johnson AB in 1947. (George Kroman)

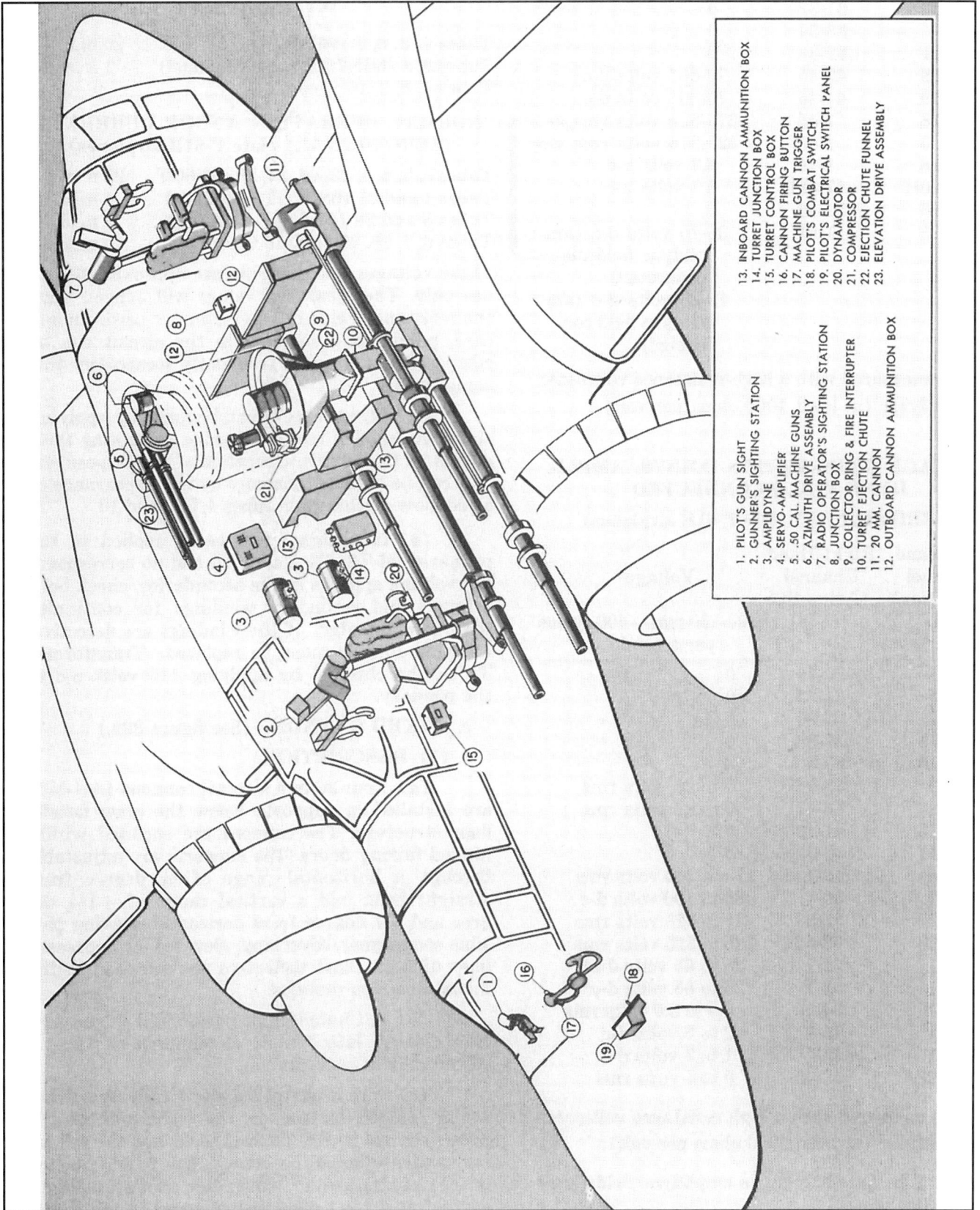

1. PILOT'S GUN SIGHT
2. GUNNER'S SIGHTING STATION
3. AMPLIDYNE
4. SERVO-AMPLIFIER
5. .50 CAL. MACHINE GUNS
6. AZIMUTH DRIVE ASSEMBLY
7. RADIO OPERATOR'S SIGHTING STATION
8. JUNCTION BOX
9. COLLECTOR RING & FIRE INTERRUPTER
10. TURRET EJECTION CHUTE
11. 20 MM. CANNON
12. OUTBOARD CANNON AMMUNITION BOX
13. INBOARD CANNON AMMUNITION BOX
14. TURRET JUNCTION BOX
15. TURRET CONTROL BOX
16. CANNON FIRING BUTTON
17. MACHINE GUN TRIGGER
18. PILOT'S COMBAT SWITCH
19. PILOT'S ELECTRICAL SWITCH PANEL
20. DYNAMOTOR
21. COMPRESSOR
22. EJECTION CHUTE FUNNEL
23. ELEVATION DRIVE ASSEMBLY

Only a cutaway drawing could reveal the destructive power that the Black Widow possessed within its ominous frame. The .50-caliber turret weighed in at over 1,500 pounds and the 20MM cannon at 150 pounds each. Both the gunner's station and the radar operator's compartment had sighting stations for the guns.

A panoramic view of the "Gun Room" at Northrop. Both the Browning .50-caliber machine guns and the 20mm cannon are pictured. Each of these guns was completely checked, tested and rechecked before they were installed in the P-61 airframes that were rolling down the assembly line. There were very few problems with any of the guns when they reached the forward areas. (Roy Wolford)

Close up view of the 20mm gun barrels with all of the access panels closed. These guns threw out a long stream of flame when they were fired, but they were underneath the aircraft and posed no danger to the aircrews' night vision. (Northrop)

An excellent shot of what it was like to work the guns in the forward combat areas. This picture shows two armorer/gunners, part of the 6th Night Fighter Squadron in the Pacific, loading the 20MM ammunition in one of the Black Widows on Saipan. These men had duel jobs, not only did they load them, they also fired them. (USAF files)

(text continued from page 64) to be moved up to a A-1-A and with the demand brought about by the Boeing contracts for B-29 production, it was not to be. So even if there had been no problem at Northrop, there might have been some difficulty in obtaining turrets for P-61 production lines.

When the production lines changed over to turretless P-61s, it ended up that most of the A model were without turrets and about the first half of the P-61B production was the same. The

An armorer from one of the night fighter squadrons in the Pacific makes some adjustments on the .50-caliber guns before putting the cover back on. This aircraft is loaded and ready for the upcoming night's mission. (USAF Files)

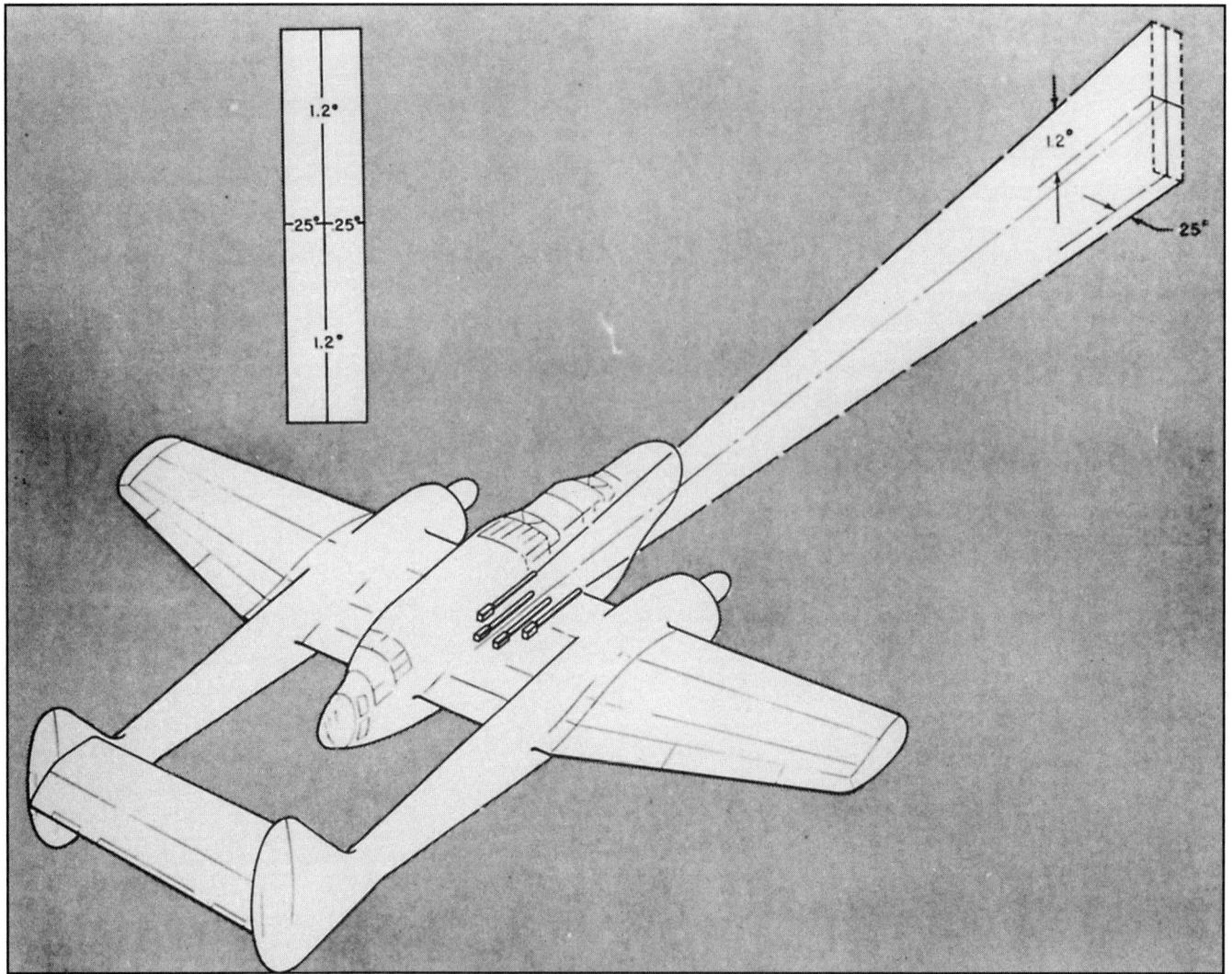

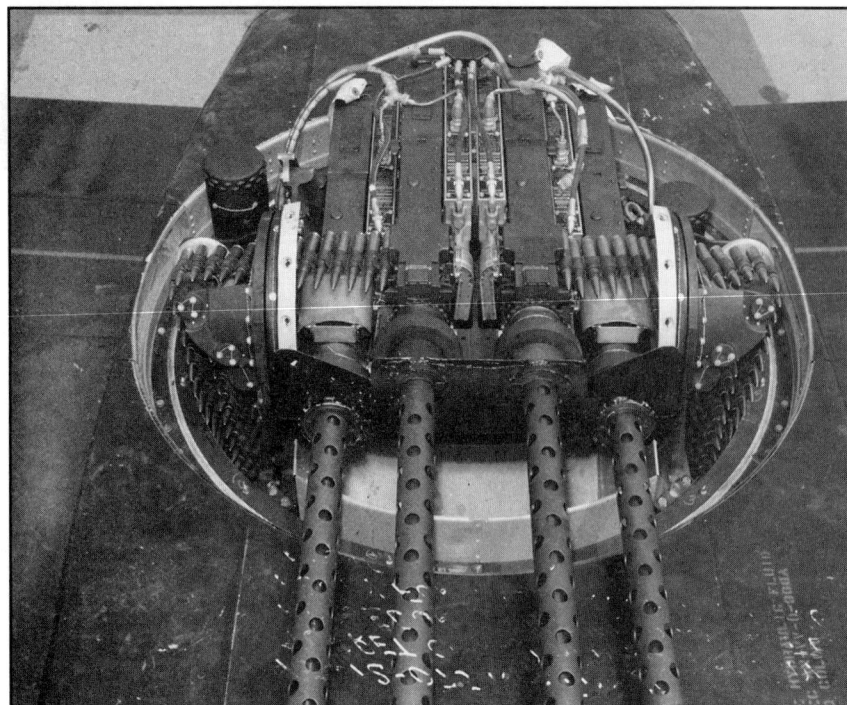

(Above) A vivid illustration demonstrating the cone of fire from the Black Widow's 20MM cannon. On a couple of missions, P-61 ace from the European Theatre, Herman Ernst claimed that when he had set up behind German aircraft from about 1,500- to 2,000-foot range, the impact from his 20MM rounds hit the inner wing roots on both sides of the enemy's fuselage. (Northrop)

With the cover of the turret removed, the complexity of the guns and firing mechanisms can be noted. General Electric had done an outstanding job in the design and reliability of the system. The B-29 gunners enjoyed many confirmed kills against Japanese fighters with these turrets. (Gerald Balzer)

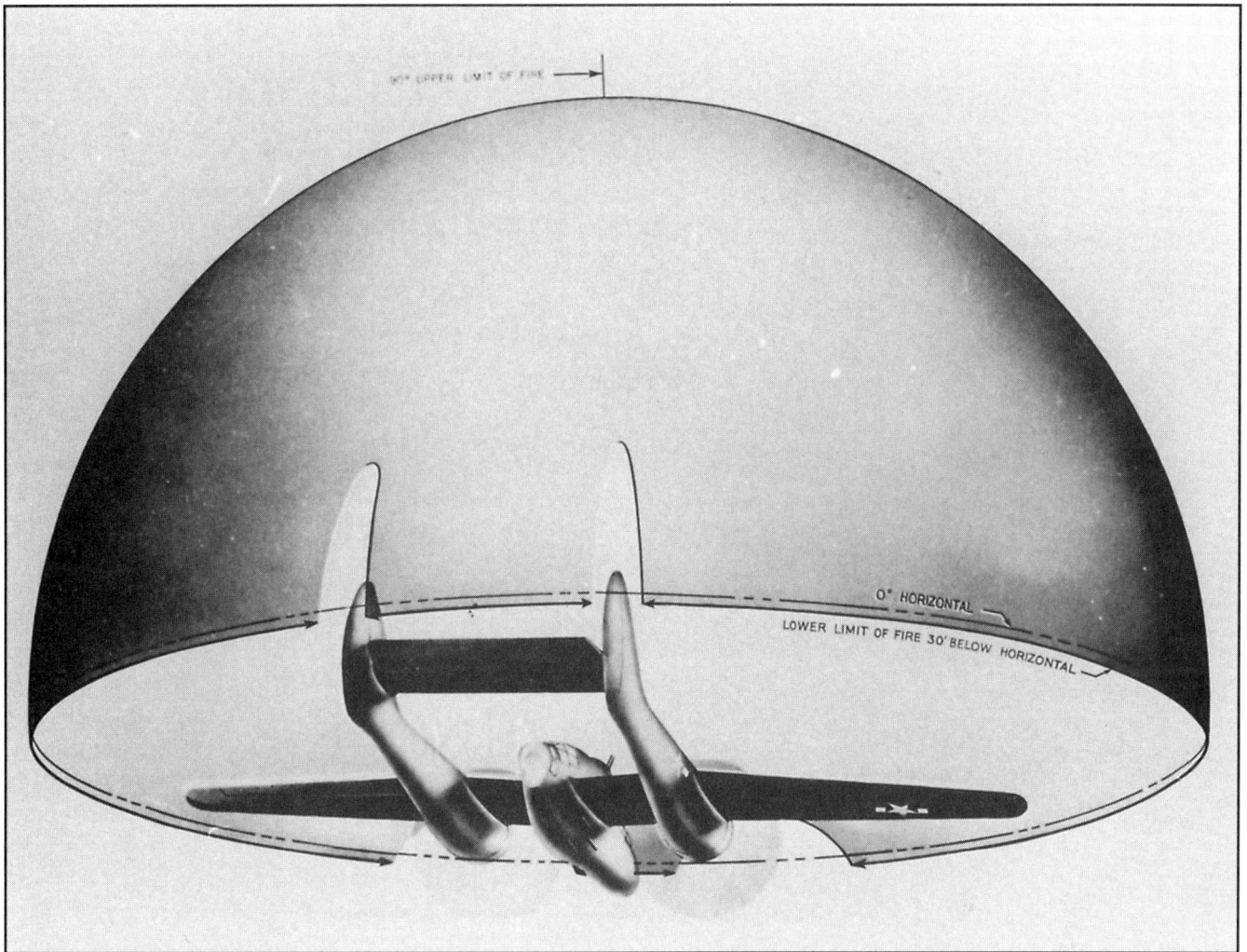

This illustration shows the versatility of the .50-caliber turret on the Black Widow. The buffeting problem eliminated some of the wide scope of fire, but it still gave the Black Widow plenty of punch at angles other than straight-away. Note the cut-out areas that prevented the guns from hitting the props or the vertical stabilizers. (Northrop)

first 37 production As to come off the assembly line had the turrets. Since a significant percentage of Black Widows going to the combat areas did not have the machine guns, then it is important to learn as much about the 20MM cannons as possible, because they would bring down more enemy aircraft than the original combination.

The four 20MM guns were installed in supports directly below the crew nacelle floor structure and they were enclosed within hinged fairing doors. The supports were adjustable through a horizontal range of one-quarter degree from dead ahead and a vertical range of one-quarter degree from horizontal, making possible converging, diverging, elevated or depressed lines of fire. These degrees were so small that at 1,500 feet range from a target, the pattern would be almost like firing dead ahead.

The firing of these weapons was controlled electrically by a firing switch button mounted on the right side of the pilot's control wheel. The guns could not be fully activated unless the nose gears doors were closed. In other words, the chances of the guns firing accidentally while the aircraft was parked was slight to none.

The cannon were manually charged on the ground only. Each cannon was provided with a 200-round maximum capacity ammunition box. Inboard ammo boxes were located just behind the forward wing spar in the crew nacelle and were accessible from the gunner's compartment. The outboard boxes were of the drawer type and were inserted through doors on the outside of the crew nacelle below both inner wings.

A Northrop engineer makes some minor adjustments to the .50-caliber turret before one of the test pilots take the aircraft up. Note the three other P-61s parked close by on the Northrop ramp. More than likely, these aircraft were being used for some final testing before changes were made on the production lines, which at this time were going strong. (Roy Wolford)

For each cannon, there was a hydraulically operated ejection chute door in the cannon access doors. The door was automatically controlled by means of a solenoid wired into the cannon firing circuit so that the doors opened only during the time the cannon were being fired. A delayed closing action was obtained by means of an adjustable restrictor valve in the hydraulic line above the cannons. This restrictor had to be adjusted so that the minimum closing time for the fastest closing door was at five to eight seconds. An ejection chute was attached to each cannon extended to each of the doors.

As for the machine guns, a description of the .50-caliber firing apparatus is given in the original "Erection and Maintenance Manual" #AN 01-15FB-2 dated March 25, 1944. "The system consists of a turret located in the upper deck of the aircraft, carrying four Browning machine

One of the P-61B models that were produced later on shows the flash eliminators installed and the guns at full vertical range. This maneuver did not cause the severe buffeting that occurred when the turret swiveled right or left. (Northrop)

WARBIRD**TECH**
S E R I E S

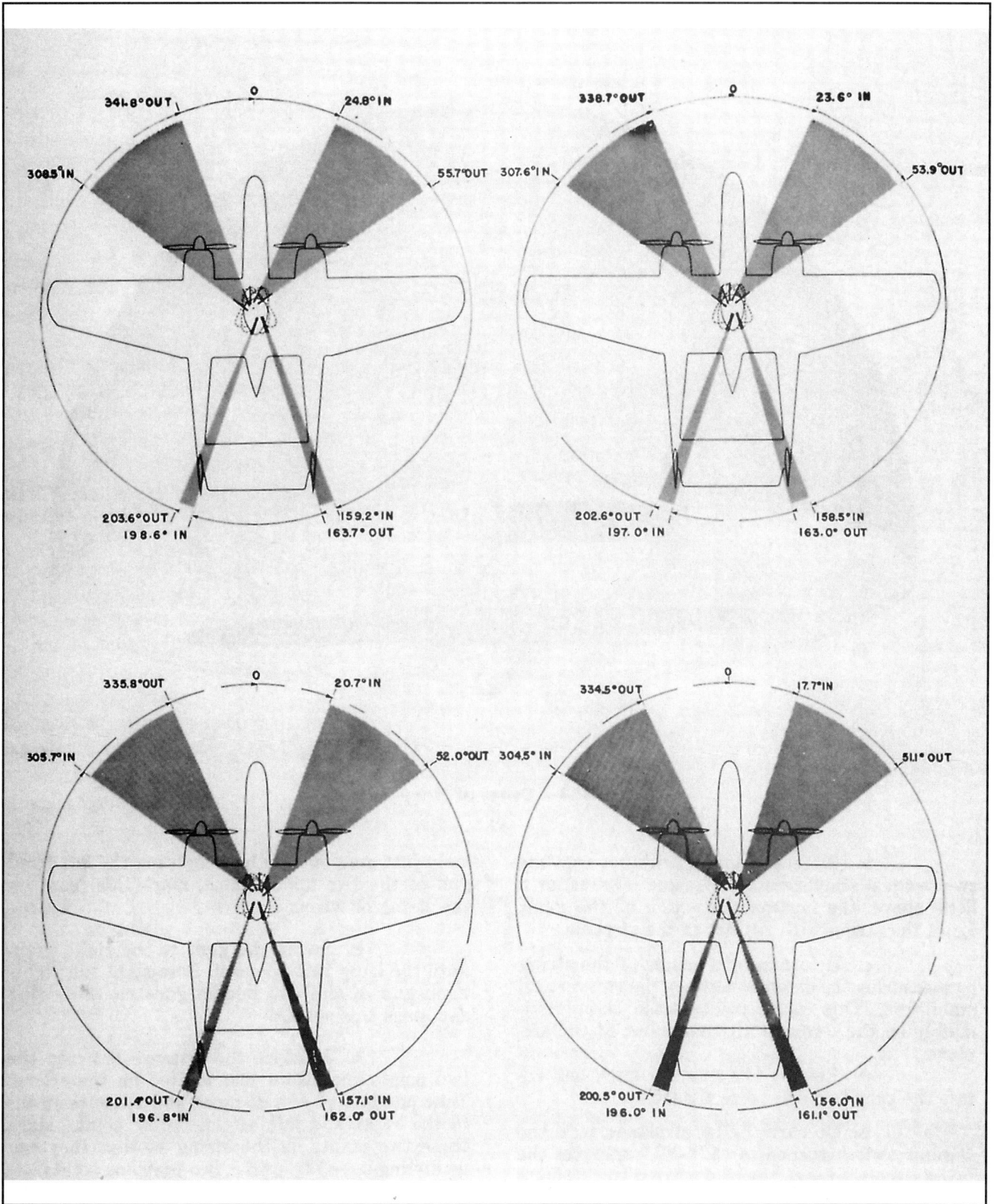

341.8° OUT   0   24.8° IN
308.5° IN
55.7° OUT
203.6° OUT   159.2° IN
198.6° IN   163.7° OUT

338.7° OUT   0   23.6° IN
307.6° IN
53.9° OUT
202.6° OUT   158.5° IN
197.0° IN   163.0° OUT

335.8° OUT   0   20.7° IN
305.7° IN
52.0° OUT
201.4° OUT   157.1° IN
196.8° IN   162.0° OUT

334.5° OUT   0   17.7° IN
304.5° IN
51.1° OUT
200.5° OUT   156.0° IN
196.0° IN   161.1° OUT

This series of diagrams show the areas in which the .50-caliber guns would not fire. To set these patterns was a very complex procedure that required adjustment of the fire interrupter switches. Fire clearance over the tail surfaces had to be precisely at + or - 2 degrees, 30 minutes. The clearance over the propellers had to be at four inches: 2 degrees, 30 minutes (+1 degree; -1/2 degree).

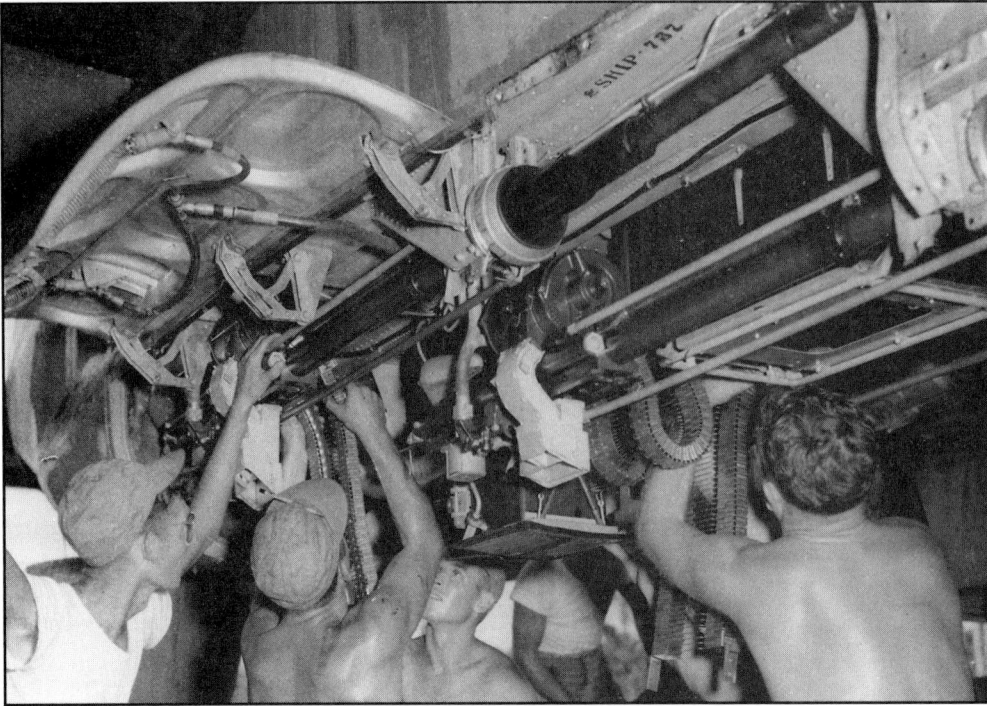

The design, testing and training was over and the time had come to execute the plan. These members of the 419th NFS are loading the 20mm cannon in one of their P-61s on Guadalcanal. This was taken in the summer of 1944, prior to the 419th earning the first of its five confirmed kills. (USAF)

guns, caliber .50 M2. These guns fire simultaneously, each at the rate of approximately 800 rounds per minute. The turret has full 360 degrees of rotation in azimuth, that is in the horizontal plane, and 90 degrees of rotation in elevation. Thus, the guns cover the full hemispheric space above the aircraft."

The rotation of the turret was electrically controlled from two sighting stations located forward and aft of the turret. The gunner in each of the sighting stations and the pilot could control the firing of the guns. The forward gunner had full control of the turret at all times unless he chose to transfer the control to the crew member in the rear compartment. He could also transfer control to the pilot after rotating the guns to a directly forward position and locking the turret.

Technicians assemble the radar units that will be fitted into the nose section of the P-61. The SCR-720 was state-of-the-art in 1942. From 1942 through 1960, more progress was made on radar than any other facet of aerial warfare, which was manifested in such all-weather jet interceptors as the F-86D, F-89 and F-102. (Northrop)

TYPICAL TARGET MARK
ALLOWS 1.5 MIL TOLERANCE

10

5

.75

1.50

6.80

3.40

2.50

8.31

16.62

TURRET GUNS
STRAFING POSITION

NIGHT BINOCULAR
RETICLE MARKS
USE INBOARD DOTS

8.85

.70

8.85

7.67

1.34

PILOT'S SIGHT FOR
0° 30' ELEVATION

LEVEL GUNSIGHT LEVEL
INDICATOR

ELEVATE TARGET TO
THIS MARK.

52.50

46.88

45.38

NOTE:

PLACE TARGET 843 INCHES
AHEAD OF FORWARD
PLUMB BOB POINT

GUN CAMERA MARKS
USE CAMERA DIM. 45.38
WITH FINDER HAVING
CROSS HAIR ¼ DISTANCE
FROM TOP OF FRAME
OPENING

USE 97.75 WITH FINDER
HAVING CROSS HAIRS
CENTERED

33.0

16.50

20 M.M. CANNON MARKS

97.75

8.50

17.0

PLUMB BOB

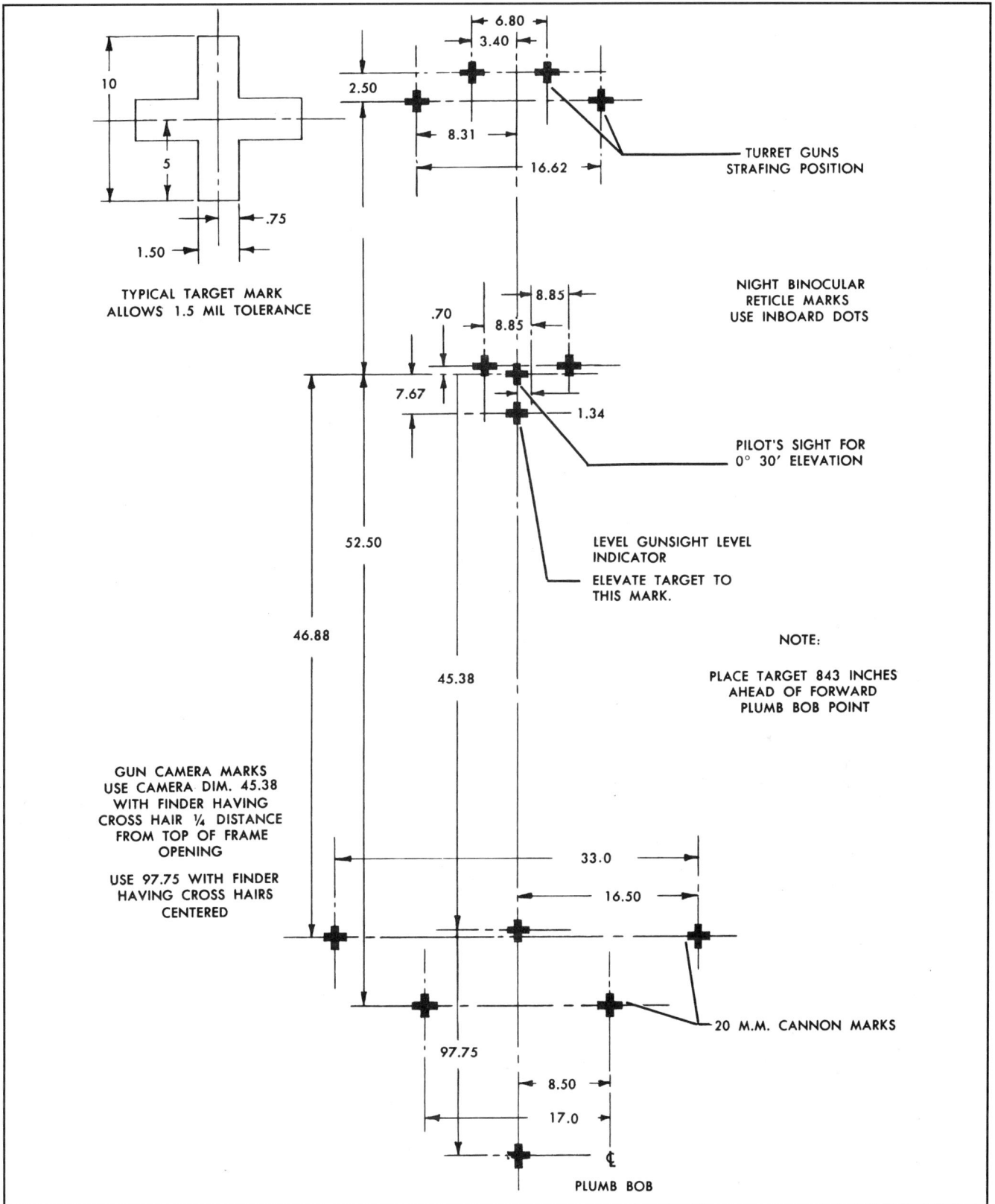

One of the most complicated jobs involved with the P-61 was boresighting its guns. The aircraft was placed on jacks and leveled up before the procedure could begin. Everything was laid out in inches, because that's how precise the guns had to be focussed. If these figures were not completely accurate, the Black Widow would not score hits on targets that were out at maximum range.

NORTHROP'S HOT RODS

The two most glaring weaknesses of the early P-61 models were lack of power and altitude limitations. The A engine was supercharged by a single-stage, gear-driven supercharger. The Bs had a few improvements, but most of them were not related directly to advantages in a combat situation. The new models had improvements such as a more dependable heater, new gun cameras and internal fire extinguishers.

However, the most important P-61B combat improvement was two-stage, gear-driven superchargers. The pilot manually shifted gears from one stage to the next by operating levers, one for each engine,

located low on the left side of the cockpit. Normally, the shift occurred when the aircraft had reached its critical altitude. The second stage increased the critical altitude by several thousand feet.

The night-flying Japanese bombers flew their missions at the maximum altitude for their aircraft and on many occasions that was sufficient to stay out of harm's way. However, the P-61B pushed them and these aircraft were able to make a few high-altitude kills.

These improvements caused the P-61B to pick up weight, to the extent that its stall speed was increased to 95 MPH. Most of the

bases that the night fighter squadrons were operating out of were long enough to accommodate this, though, and the slower landing speeds were not necessary.

The next design improvement was the big P-61C with its supercharged R-2800-73 Pratt & Whitney engines, which developed about 2,100 horsepower each for takeoff. This power was attached to two four-blade paddle props. All of these features and two large air scoops under each engine accommodated the General Electric turbo superchargers, making it a powerful machine.

Max R. Stanley, a veteran Northrop

A three-quarter frontal from the right side of the third production P-61C (#43-8323) to come off the assembly line. With its wide paddle props and air scoops, the C was a much more ominous looking fighter than the earlier models. (Gerald Balzer)

An excellent frontal view of a P-61C with all four 310-gallon external tanks attached. With the addition of this fuel capacity, the range more than doubled. Had the C been fortunate enough to work in a combat area, it would have had plenty of loiter time. (Northrop)

test pilot, states, "The P-61C engines were retrofitted with turbo superchargers. The new retrofit was accomplished by Goodyear in Akron, Ohio. This new engine configuration greatly improved the altitude performance of the fighter. Test flights at 40,000 feet were commonplace. The normal O.A.T. was about a minus 56 degrees F. at those altitudes. The P-61 cockpit was not pressurized and a suitable cabin heater did not exist. Hence, the P-61C was wired to accommodate the electric heated flight suits worn by the crew."

A close up view of the new fighter brakes installed in the outer wings of the P-61C. These were added at the request of the AAF because of the aircraft's increased speed. (Roy Wolford)

An XP-61D closeup shows the propeller cuff extensions. This was the first (ship #791) of two P-61A conversions into the experimental D models. Both were powered by the Pratt & Whitney R-2800-77 engine. (Northrop)

One specific feature built into the C made it very different from the A and B—the fighter brake. A brake was installed in each outer wing that consisted of extensible panels in the upper and lower surfaces of the wing, similar to dive brakes.

According to Northrop pilot Stanley: "The fighter brakes were designed and installed on a test P-61 to meet a requirement established by the Air Force. The function of this device was to enable a pilot in a tail-chase attack to reduce air speed rapidly to prevent an over-run and to avoid the hunter

The XP-61E was designed to be the long-range fighter escort for the B-29 missions to Japan. This cockpit shot shows the left side of the cockpit in ship #2. This was taken after it had been totalled in a takeoff accident. (Gerald Balzer)

The second of two XP-61Ds (Ship #819) was involved in some extensive ground tests, in this case, reverse prop tests. Because of excessive use of the brakes and the heat it produced, the main gear's tires failed. (Northrop)

becoming the hunted! Flight tests confirmed their effectiveness."

The fighter brakes could not be operated unless the landing gear was locked in the up position. A spring-loaded, toggle switch mounted on the fire extinguisher switch panel overrides the fighter brake safety switch circuit to allow the brakes to be tested while the aircraft is on the ground.

Perhaps the most dangerous test flight made in any model of the P-61 was flown by test pilot Stanley, who recalls the details: "At the insistence of the Air Force, the final test was scheduled as a 'structural integrity demonstration.' This test required the pilot to apply maximum Gs at the maximum permissible air speed at the critical Mach number. This dictated performing

the maneuver at 17,000 feet.

"It was at this time I activated the brakes. When I applied back pressure on the stick to produce the desired Gs, I found the stick force had reduced to zero. The stick ended up in my lap and the last thing I recall is noting the accelerometer pegged at 10 Gs! The aircraft was greatly overstressed; both wings and empennage failed, structurally, and separated from the airplane. This produced negative Gs to the extent that I was pitched forward with such force that the pilot's seat pulled free from its attach points on the floor. My face struck the windscreen and my oxygen mask absorbed the effects of this blow."

Stanley managed to unlatch the top of the canopy and was thrown

out the top by the forces. He parachuted to safety. Fortunately, no one else was in the aircraft when the test was flown.

"Subsequent flight tests confirmed the basic cause of my experience was the phenomenon of 'compressibility' about which very little was known at the time. No effort was made to find a solution to the problem. All P-61s coming off the line at that time had fighter brakes installed. However, they had been rendered inoperative and bolted closed. P-61 fighter brakes were never used in combat," Stanley said.

Basically, the C model was exactly what the pilots had been asking for. It would have encountered no equal in the skies over Europe or Japan. There was one major problem though, World War II ended

The guns were shifted to the nose on the XP-61E because the dorsal turret was eliminated. In this picture, the four .50-caliber machine guns are set up for testing in the nose section destined for ship #2. (Northrop)

before they saw combat. Only 41 of these magnificent P-61C airframes were built, and the final aircraft was accepted on January 28, 1946.

The P-61C had been on the drawing boards for quite some time, and as far back as September 1943, the government had committed for a total of 80. One year later, this total had been reduced to 67, and the end of the war stopped that figure short.

Northrop's engineers and designers had been extremely busy during the latter half of 1944 and early 1945, with projects that went far beyond the P-61C. Once this model was in production, the engineers took it up one more notch with the XP-61D.

This experiment involved two P-61A airframes (#42-5559 and #42-5587). The XP-61D was truly a hot rod of a fighter, at least on the drawing board. These two

The cockpit layout for the XP-61E shows the position for the co-pilot/navigator in the back seat. This arrangement allowed the aircraft to be able to fly the very long missions to Japan with two pilots on-board. (Northrop)

This is all that remained of this P-61C after test pilot Max Stanley took it up to test the fighter brakes in a Structural Integrity demonstration. Stanley managed to bail out as the wings and tail came off after a main wing spar failed. The test was ordered by the AAF, and it was executed at the required 17,000 feet. Note that the wings and tail are missing.(Northrop)

conversions called for the Pratt and Whitney R-2800-77 engines with General Electric CH-5 turbo chargers (identical to those being used on the B-29). The speed had been pegged at 430 MPH at 30,000 feet, and the service ceiling had been elevated to 41,000 feet.

The XP- 61D was tested in early November 1944, and unfortunately, it was all downhill from there. Tests determined that performance had not improved substantially over the C. With the overall improvement in performance lacking, funding dried up quickly.

By the late fall of 1944, it was no secret that the war in the Pacific

was going very well for the Allies. It was just a matter of months before the Japanese homeland would be exposed to the same devastation that had been dealt on the islands leading to Japan. The build-up of American forces in the Pacific could not be stopped.

The B-29 would have the responsibility of taking the war to the heart of Japan. Its long-range capability made it the weapon of choice. But, there was a slight weakness in this plan. The bombers needed fighter protection while they were over Japan and the United States did not have a fighter with that range. Hence, Northrop went to work to come up with an aircraft that could

provide the legs for the mission, a long-range, heavily armed fighter escort with exceptional performance characteristics.

It should be noted that earlier in 1944, the Army Air Corps had given a contract to North American, the manufacturer of the P-51 Mustang, to work on a long-range fighter escort that was officially known as the XP-82.

This concept provided the seed that developed into the XP-61E long-range fighter, which involved the conversion of two P-61B airframes (#42-39549 and #42-39557). The original concept behind this idea was very sound and it had the

An outstanding picture of the XP-61E (ship #1) in-flight over Los Angeles in 1945. This aircraft survived the doomed "E" tests and was shifted over to the XF-15 Reconnaissance program. (Roy Wolford)

XP-61E Ship #2 waits for the salvage crews to haul it away. On this test flight, the test pilot pulled the gear up too soon, causing the aircraft to settle down on the runway, bending the props and totalling it out. Originally, this '61E was a modified P-61B-10 (#42-39557). (Gerald Balzer)

attention of most Air Corps planners. In appearance, this airframe was different from the A, B and C models. The top of the crew nacelle had been cut off and in its place was a long clear bubble canopy. There was a crew of two, with a pilot in front and a co-pilot/navigator behind the pilot.

The top turret had been eliminated from the E. However, there was no loss of firepower because the four .50-caliber machine guns had been moved up into the nose section. Each of these guns would have 300 rounds of ammunition. The four 20MM cannon were still intact in the ventral underside of the crew nacelle. The void left by removal of the turret was filled by

The first of two XP-61E long-range fighter escorts is viewed from an unusual position. The clean lines are especially prominent from this angle. Note the guns in the nose were in a box configuration, which was the easiest way to discern between ship #1 and ship #2. (Gerald Balzer)

A close-up side view of the 310-gallon drop tank that has been fitted with fins for stability. The tests were performed on this early production P-61A (#719). These tanks were a vital asset to the P-61C and D performance. Note that the lettering on the tank states, "U.S. Air Force". The official recognition of this branch of the military was still over a year away. (Gerald Balzer)

Close-up view of the earliest version of the fighter brakes that had been installed on test ship #719 (P-61A). (Gerald Balzer)

additional fuel tanks and radio equipment.

Due to the distance that the bombing missions would require, fuel capacity was of the utmost importance. With the additional fuel provided in the crew nacelle (518 gallons) and 640 gallons in the wing tanks, the total fuel available from internal tanks was 1,158 gallons. With its ability to carry four 310-gallon tanks externally, the added capacity pushed its combat range to almost 4,000 miles, which was sufficient to stay with the B-29s on their bombing missions over Japan.

The two XP-61E models were almost identical to the naked eye, but there were two distinct differences. In the A/C# 42-39549, which was the first conversion, the bubble canopy was hinged on the left side and swung open to the left. Also, the guns on '549 were arranged in a two-on-top-of-two (box) configuration. On the second aircraft, #42-39557, the canopy was on rails and slid backward when opened, and the .50-caliber guns

Top view of the induction system that was from the intercooler to the carburetor in the Pratt & Whitney R-2800-77 engine. This was taken of the left engine on the XP-61D. (Northrop)

WARBIRDTECH
SERIES

The remains of the P-61C that was undergoing the high G fighter brakes demonstration. Max Stanley, the test pilot, was lucky to have been able to exit the aircraft. Note the the wings and tail are missing. Stanley said that the airframe had pulled 10 Gs before it came apart. (Northrop)

in the nose were arranged in a horizontal set (four across).

Needless to say, these two airframes did not have much of a future. Number 557 was only about 30 days into its test phase, on April 11, 1945, when it hit a serious obstacle. The aircraft was beginning a maximum performance takeoff and the pilot retracted the gear too early. The aircraft settled down and the props hit the runway, which totalled out XP-61E #2. The remaining ship was converted over to the F-15 Reconnaissance program as the XF-15.

It wasn't the end of World War II, though, that hastened the night fighter's demise as much as the jet age. Northrop had developed a fantastic airplane with unlimited potential—if the prop jobs had had a future. The beginning of the all-jet Air Force was already in the works and the Russians were just starting to crank up the long Cold War. This 40-year war would drive technology forward into the Space Age, rendering numerous aircraft designs and weapons obsolete.

In sheer speculation, having studied the Korean War for many years, it would be interesting to imagine what some aircraft types would have done if they had been involved in the action. If the P-61C or P-61D aircraft had gone into mass production and had been in active service during 1950, it might have been called into combat during the early days of the Korean War and would have done a very credible job.

The '61 would have excelled in night intruder work, as the B-26 and F7F did. Loiter time, payload and radar capability would have made them effective in night interdiction and close air support. The F-82 came through when it was called upon during the early weeks, but the jets and lack of parts drove it out of service. The P-61 would have suffered the same fate. Still, it is interesting to imagine what could have been.

The Final 7 Chapter

The Jet Age Cuts the Widow's Career Short

When World War II ended, the Black Widow's door to the future was slammed shut. It was that simple, and although the P-61 hung around for a few more years, it had no funding and very low priority. It was a stop-gap that did not survive long in the post-war era. It was even replaced before the jets had become entrenched, by the North American F-82 Twin Mustang.

Northrop would not give up. It breathed a few more breaths into the P-61 by signing a contract to convert some of the unfinished airframes into the F-15 (RF-61C) Photo Reconnaissance aircraft. The only remaining XP-61E was brought back into the plant and had cameras placed in its nose section and all of its guns removed. This ship became officially known as the XF-15. The Air Force planners deter-

Shady Lady was a P-61 assigned to the 319th All-Weather Squadron operating out of Rio Hato AB, Panama. Before moving back to the United States, the squadron was stationed at both France AB, Canal Zone, and Rio Hato. (Joe Cuthbert)

An F-15A Reporter, from the 8th Photo Recon Squadron, takes on fuel before continuing its mission of photo mapping remote islands in the Pacific. This was taken in 1948 on Zamboanga. (Tony Linkiewicz)

mined that they would need over 300 of these aircraft and immediately awarded a contract for 175.

The first ship to roll off the assembly lines did so in September 1946. By this time, the Air Force had realized that the jet age technology was taking over and if we were to keep pace with any potential adversaries, it would have to be with an airframe that could move very fast. The contract was cancelled in 1947, and only 36 of the F-15s saw the light of day. The RF-80A was to be the heir apparent for that mission.

(Above) The 319th All-Weather Squadron flew the P-61 out of bases in Panama. This picture shows the elaborate nose art that adorned some of their Black Widows during this period. This squadron would eventually move up to McChord AFB and then Moses Lake AFB. From there they would take their F-94Bs into combat in Korea. (Norman Goldsobel)

The guns had just been removed and the new cameras installed in the XF-15. Due to government cutbacks, less than 40 of these Reporters were built. The Air Force determined that the future of long-range reconnaissance was in the hands of the jets. (Garry Pape)

One of the more colorful F-15s assigned to the 8th Photo Recon Squadron at Johnson Air Base, Japan, was assigned to pilot Lieutenant Tony Linkiewicz. The 8th was the only operational squadron to use the F-15A (RF-61C). (USAF)

Four P-61Cs and one F-15A line up to attack a thunderstorm that was moving into the area. This was taken at the Wilmington, Ohio, airport and the aircraft were part of Operation Thunderstorm. Note the damaged nose of the lead ship caused by hail encountered in the storms. (USAF)

WARBIRDTECH
SERIES

A rare shot of P-61B (#42-39754) in-flight during 1947 to '48. It was based out of Cleveland, Ohio, and was being operated at NACA's Lewis Flight Propulsion Laboratory. It test flew airfoil ramjets. (Garry Pape)

From 1947 through 1948, the F-15A Reporter did an excellent job photomapping most of the countries and islands in the Far East. This job was given to the only Air Force squadron to operate the

A flight of four F-15As en route to Clark AB in the Philippines. Their mission was to photo map the numerous islands in the area, including the Philippine Islands. This was taken in January 1948. (Tony Lickiewicz)

In 1980, this P-61C was still waiting restoration at the Smithsonian storage facility. The other existing P-61 in the United States has been restored and is currently on display at the Air Force Museum in Dayton, Ohio. (Robert Drake)

The seventeenth production F-15A is parked on the ramp at Johnson Air Base, Japan. It was flown by the 8th Photo Recon as noted by the "8-Ball" symbol on the crew nacelle. This was taken on July 7, 1947 during the very early stages of the 8th's photo mapping mission. (USAF)

WARBIRDTECH
S E R I E S

One of the last P-61Cs to be accepted by the Air Force. (#43-8356) was used extensively during the Operation Thunderstorm project. The data that was obtained by these flights into the storm fronts gained valuable information not only for the military but also for the airlines. (Peter M. Bowers)

F-15, the 8th Photo Reconnaissance Squadron that was attached to the 35th Fighter Group out of Johnson Air Base, Japan. There would be a total of 27 of these aircraft sent to the Far East for this role.

One of the 8th Photo Recon F-15s is subjected to the bitter cold winters that are experienced in northern Japan during the winter of 1947 and '48. (Clarence Wiklund)

One of the most publicized P-61s to come out of World War II was Lady in the Dark. This 548th NFS Black Widow was probably responsible for the final kill of the war, when it forced a Japanese fighter to crash into the water in a high-speed chase late on the night that the war ended. This photo was taken in 1948 at Clark Air Base's boneyard. (Guy Razzeto)

The final resting place for these former 548th NFS Black Widows was to be in a burial pit at Clark Air Base. These aircraft were stripped of all useable parts by maintenance crews from the 4th All Weather Squadron on Okinawa. They were desperately trying to keep their P-61s in service. (Guy Razzeto)

WARBIRDTECH
S E R I E S

If this scene existed today, you would be looking at several million dollars worth of airframes. But, in 1948, you were looking at discarded aircraft that were not worth hauling back to the United States for scrap. All of the Black Widows in this picture were ex-548th NFS. A pitiful end for such a great fighter! (Guy Razzeto)

Probably the most significant contribution the F-15 made to the military in its post-war role was when it photo mapped the entire South Korean peninsula. The maps created by this project were the only ones available when the Korean War broke out in June 1950. The information was invaluable, and these maps were not upgraded until a detachment of Marine F7F-3P Tigercats went in to take up-to-date pictures of Inchon Harbor in preparation for the famous Inchon Landing.

A shot of the XF-15A during the initial test flight over the mountains of California. (Ira Chart/Northrop)

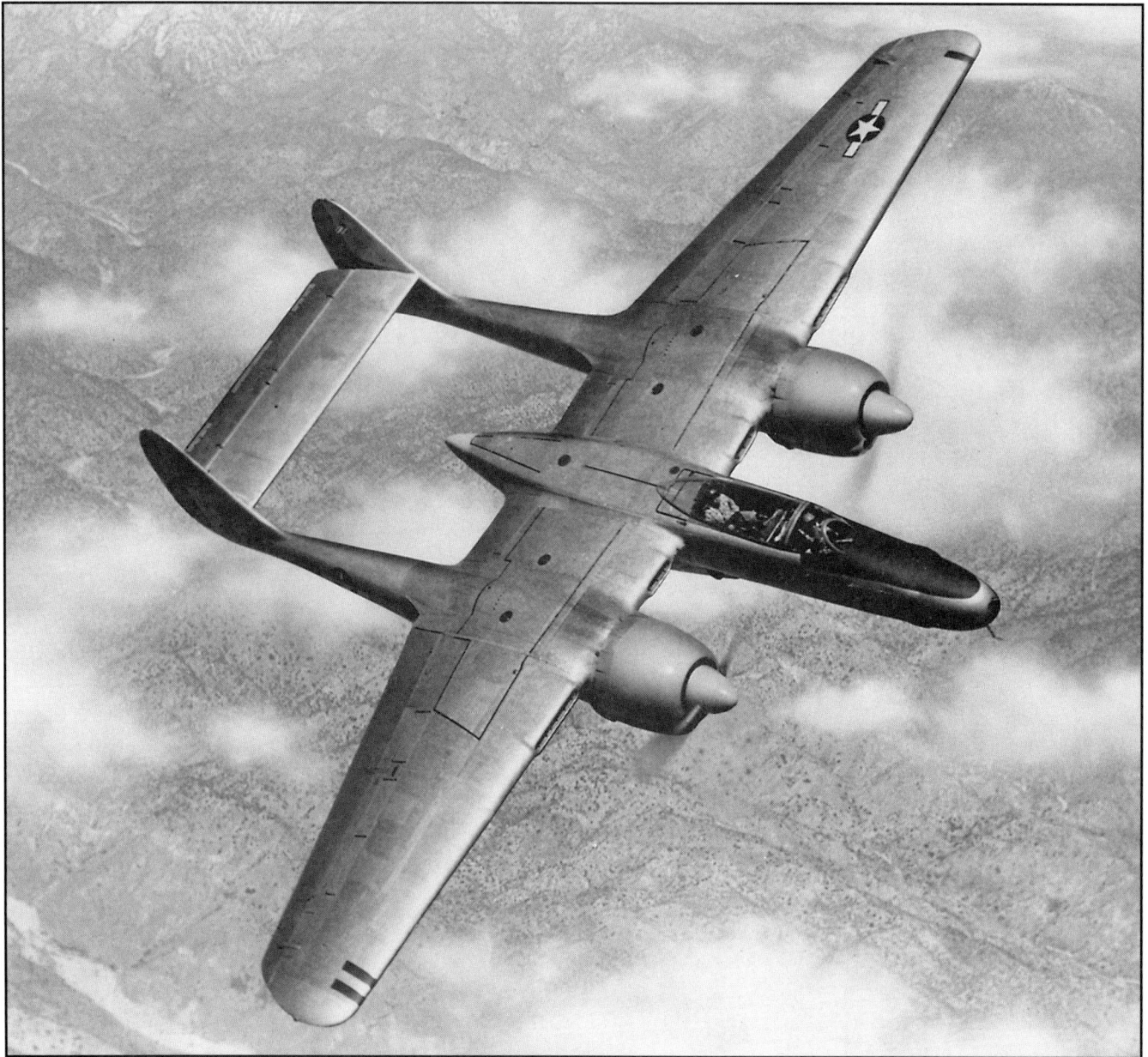

A beautiful picture of the XF-15A during a test flight over the California desert. This was a P-61C that was converted. (Ira Chart/Northrop)

In the latter half of 1945 and throughout 1946, the remaining Black Widows were the aircraft of choice to fill the all-weather role. After all, there were no replacements ready to step in, yet there was no real threat because the Russians were still trying to pick up the pieces from the war and reorganize their war machine.

The P-61Bs were placed in front-line squadrons in Japan, Okinawa, United States, Panama, Alaska and Germany. There was no glamour in the all-weather business during this time, and keeping these aircraft in top shape with a good in-service rate was not on the list of priorities for the Air Force. The available monies were channeled into getting the all-jet force up and running.

In 1948, the rate that P-61s were being sent to the bone yard was steadily increasing as F-82s came off the assembly line. It was not an embarrassment for the Black Widow to be replaced by another prop aircraft. It was just the fact that the Twin Mustangs were newer and would be cheaper to maintain until the F-94s were ready to go operational. Three years later, the F-82s met the same fate.

One of only two surviving P-61Cs is shown here during its early days at the Air Force Museum in Dayton, Ohio. Circa 1972. Ship #43-38353 has been repainted in the colors of the 550th NFS of World War II. (Garry Pape)

Frontal view of a surviving P-61C at the Air Force Museum. The only other C left is owned by the Smithsonian. (Garry Pape)

This P-61 had been converted into a fire fighter based in California. It crashed in 1963, killing the pilot. It was the last flyable Black Widow. (Bill Beavers via Victor Seely)

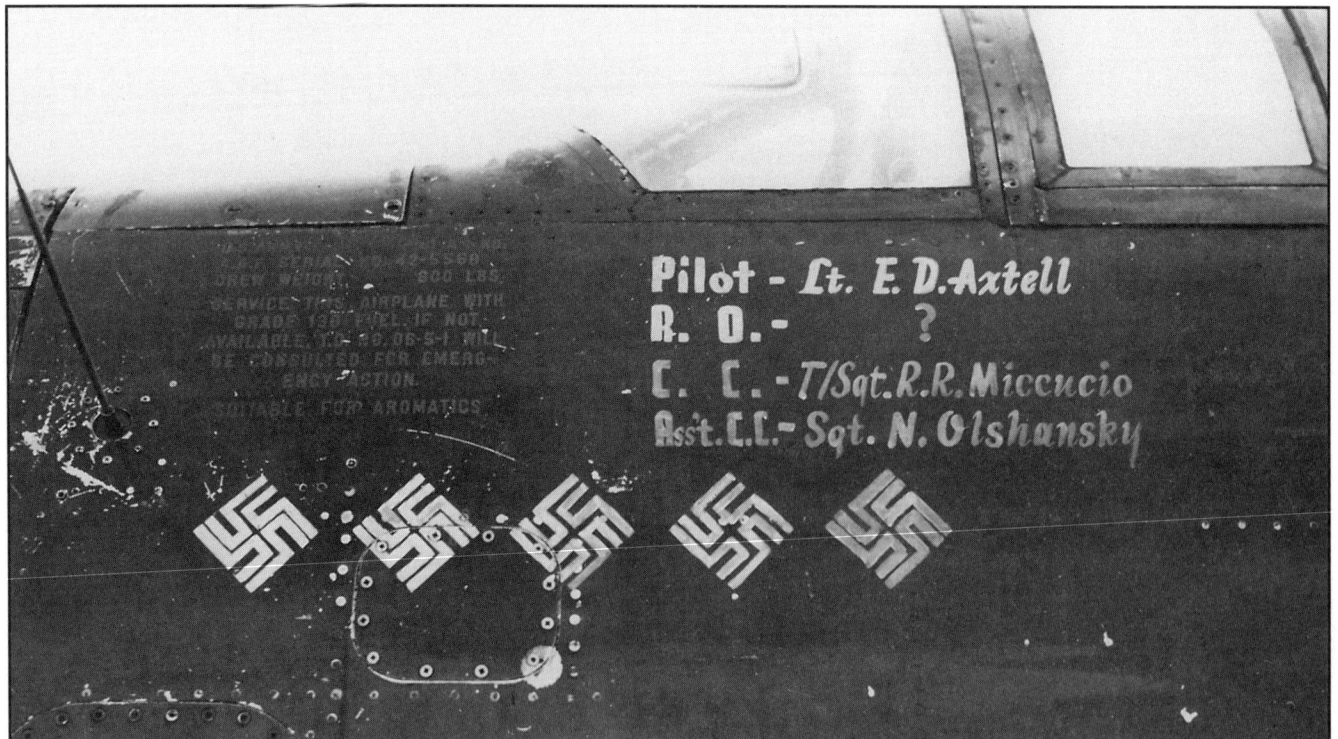

Pilot - Lt. E.D.Axtell
R. O.-   ?
C. C. - T/Sgt.R.R.Miccucio
Asst.C.C.- Sgt. N. Olshansky

Flash back to the days of glory. It has nothing to do with the waning, post-war career of the P-61, but it makes a dramatic statement. It symbolizes what the Black Widow was designed for and proof that it did live up to its name. This photograph shows a small segment of Lieutenant Eugene Axtell's P- 61A Battle Ax. Axtell was one of four aces from the 422nd Night Fighter Squadron, which led all night fighter squadrons with 43 kills. This is the picture you want to remember the Northrop P-61 Black Widow by! (John Anderson)

WARBIRDTECH
SERIES

APPENDIX

MODEL	NUMBER OF A/C	DESCRIPTION
XP-61	2	Prototypes
YP-61	13	Test & Evaluation Training
P-61A	200	First Full-Scale Production
P-61B	450	Largest Production Run
P-61C	41	Post-War Projects
XP-61D	2	Modified P-61s
XP-61E	2	Modified P-61Bs Long-Range Escort Fighter with Bubble Canopy
XP-61F	0	Modified P-61C/Project Scrubbed
P-61G	16	Modified P-61Bs: Weather Reconnaissance 1945
XF-15	1	XP-61E (Ship #2) modified
XF-15A	1	Modified P-61C
F-15A	36	Produced From Partially Completed P-61Cs
F2T-1	12	Surplus A Models Used as Night Fighter Trainers by United States Marine Corps.

SIGNIFICANT DATES

30 JANUARY 1941
The initial contract signed between Northrop and the Air Corps for two XP-61s and two wind tunnel models.

10 MARCH 1941
Contract approved for the AAC to purchase 13 YP-61s.

26 MAY 1942
The first flight of the XP-61 is flown by test pilot Vance Breese.

15 JULY 1943
Activation of the 349th Night Fighter Squadron, the first official night fighter training organization in the Army Air Corps. They would train in the P-70 and the P-61.

6 AUGUST 1943
The first of 13 YP-61s was delivered to the AAC and the final Y was delivered in September.

OCTOBER 1943
The first P-61A rolls off the assembly line. The first 37 As had the top .50-caliber turrets installed.

8 JANUARY 1944
The public was finally exposed to the top secret Black Widow when one flew over the Los Angeles Coliseum during a joint Army- Navy Show with 75,000 people in attendance.

21 MARCH 1944
P-61A-1-NO (#42-5496) was turned over to the RAF for test and evaluation. This was the 12th production P-61A.

APRIL 1944
The first P-61As started arriving at the Air Depot in Hawaii.

1 MAY 1944
The 6th Night Fighter Squadron becomes the first unit to be equipped with the Black Widow, in the Pacific. Its new A models are equipped with the dorsal .50-caliber turret.

23 MAY 1944
The 422nd Night Fighter Squadron becomes the first unit equipped with the P-61 in Europe. Their A models did not have the .50-caliber turret.

1 JUNE 1944
The 550th NFS was activated. This was the last of 16 operational combat night fighter squadrons to see time in World War II. The 550th was destined for the Pacific Theatre.

26 DECEMBER 1944
Lieutenant Paul A. Smith, of the 422nd NFS, becomes the first night fighter ace in the Black Widow.

30 DECEMBER 1944
Major Carroll C. Smith becomes the first Black Widow ace in the Pacific. He was commanding officer of the 418th NFS.

11 APRIL 1945
The second of only two prototype XP-61Es (#42-39557) was totalled in a take-off accident. This doomed the project.

3 JULY 1945
Test pilot L.A. Parrett takes the XP-61E/XF-15 up for its first flight.

28 JANUARY 1946
The forty-first P-61C was accepted by the Air Force. It was the final C to be produced for the military.

29 JUNE 1946
The first flights of Operation Thunderstorm began. This was an intense study of thunderstorms and it utilized nine P-61Cs.

SEPTEMBER 1946
The first production F-15A-1 is accepted by the Air Force.

MAY 1950
The last operational F-61 was pulled out of service in Japan, just 30 days before the Korean War started. It had already been replaced by the F-82G Twin Mustang.